THE **W**ORD ON THE LIFE OF JESUS

JIM BURNS
THE NATIONAL INSTITUTE OF YOUTH MINISTRY

Gospel Light

Gospel Light is an evangelical Christian publisher dedicated to serving the local church. We believe God's vision for Gospel Light is to provide church leaders with biblical, user-friendly materials that will help them evangelize, disciple and minister to children, youth and families.

We hope this Gospel Light resource will help you discover biblical truth for your own life and help you minister to youth. God bless you in your work.

For a free catalog of resources from Gospel Light please contact your Christian supplier or call 1-800-4-GOSPEL.

PUBLISHING STAFF

Jean Daly, Editor
Pam Weston, Editorial Assistant
Kyle Duncan, Editorial Director
Bayard Taylor, M. Div., Editor, Theological and Biblical Issues
Joey O'Connor, Contributing Writer
Mario Ricketts, Designer

ISBN 0-8307-1647-5
© 1995 Jim Burns
All rights reserved.
Printed in U.S.A.

HOW TO MAKE CLEAN COPIES FROM THIS BOOK

PRAISE FOR YOUTHBUILDERS

Jim Burns knows young people. He also knows how to communicate to them. This study should be in the hands of every youth leader interested in discipling young people.

David Adams, Vice President, Lexington Baptist College

I deeply respect and appreciate the groundwork Jim Burns has prepared for true teenage discernment. YouthBuilders is timeless in the sense that the framework has made it possible to plug into any society, at any point in time, and to proceed to discuss, experience and arrive at sincere moral and Christian conclusions that will lead to growth and life changes. Reaching young people may be more difficult today than ever before, but God's grace is alive and well in Jim Burns and this wonderful curriculum.

Fr. Angelo J. Artemas, Youth Ministry Director, Greek Orthodox Archdiocese of North and South America

I heartily recommend Jim Burns's *YouthBuilders Group Bible Studies* because they are leader-friendly tools that are ready to use in youth groups and Sunday School classes. Jim addresses the tough questions that students are genuinely facing every day and, through his engaging style, challenges young people to make their own decisions to move from their current opinions to God's convictions taught in the Bible. Every youth group will benefit from this excellent curriculum.

Paul Borthwick, Minister of Missions, Grace Chapel

Jim Burns recognizes the fact that small groups are where life change happens. In this study he has captured the essence of that value. Further, Jim has given much thought to shaping this very effective material into a usable tool that serves the parent, leader and student.

Bo Boshers, Executive Director, Student Impact,
Willow Creek Community Church

It is about time that someone who knows kids, understands kids and works with kids writes youth curriculum that youth workers, both volunteer and professional, can use. Jim Burns's *YouthBuilders Group Bible Studies* is the curriculum that youth ministry has been waiting a long time for.

Ridge Burns, President,
The Center for Student Missions

There are very few people in the world who know how to communicate life-changing truth effectively to teens. Jim Burns is one of the best. *YouthBuilders Group Bible Studies* puts handles on those skills and makes them available to everyone. These studies are biblically sound, hands-on practical and just plain fun. This one gets a five-star endorsement—which isn't bad since there are only four stars to start with.

Ken Davis, President,
Dynamic Communications

I don't know anyone who knows and understands the needs of the youth worker like Jim Burns. His new curriculum not only reveals his knowledge of youth ministry but also his depth and sensitivity to the Scriptures. *YouthBuilders Group Bible Studies* is solid, easy to use and gets students out of their seats and into the Word. I've been waiting for something like this for a long time!

Doug Fields, Pastor of High School,
Saddleback Valley Community Church

Jim Burns has a way of being creative without being "hokey." *YouthBuilders Group Bible Studies* takes the age-old model of curriculum and gives it a new look with tools such as the Bible *Tuck-In*™ and Parent Page. Give this new resource a try and you'll see that Jim shoots straightforward on tough issues. The *YouthBuilders* series is great for leading small-group discussions as well as teaching a large class of junior high or high school students. The Parent Page will help you get support from your parents in that they will understand the topics you are dealing with in your group. Put Jim's years of experience to work for you by equipping yourself with this quality material.

Curt Gibson, Pastor to Junior High,
First Church of the Nazarene of Pasadena

Once again, Jim Burns has managed to handle very timely issues with just the right touch. His *YouthBuilders Group Bible Studies* succeeds in teaching solid biblical values without being stuffy or preachy. The format is user-friendly, designed to stimulate high involvement and deep discussion. Especially impressive is the Parent Page, a long overdue tool to help parents become part of the Christian education loop. I look forward to using it with my kids!

David M. Hughes, Pastor,
First Baptist Church, Winston-Salem

What do you get when you combine a deep love for teens, over 20 years' experience in youth ministry and an excellent writer? You get Jim Burns's *YouthBuilders* series! This stuff has absolutely hit the nail on the head. Quality Sunday School and small-group material is tough to come by these days, but Jim has put every ounce of creativity he has into these books.

Greg Johnson, author of *Getting Ready for the Guy/Girl Thing* and *Keeping Your Cool While Sharing Your Faith*

Jim Burns has a gift, the gift of combining the relational and theological dynamics of our faith in a graceful, relevant and easy-to-chew-and-swallow way. *YouthBuilders Group Bible Studies* is a hit, not only for teens but for teachers.

Gregg Johnson, National Youth Director,
International Church of the Foursquare Gospel

The practicing youth worker always needs more ammunition. Here is a whole book full of practical, usable resources for those facing kids face-to-face. *YouthBuilders Group Bible Studies* will get that blank stare off the faces of kids in your youth meeting!
Jay Kesler, President, Taylor University

I couldn't be more excited about the *YouthBuilders Group Bible Studies*. It couldn't have arrived at a more needed time. Spiritually we approach the future engaged in war with young people taking direct hits from the devil. This series will practically help teens who feel partially equipped to "put on the whole armor of God."
Mike MacIntosh, Pastor,
Horizon Christian Fellowship

In *YouthBuilders Group Bible Studies*, Jim Burns pulls together the key ingredients for an effective curriculum series. Jim captures the combination of teen involvement and a solid biblical perspective, with topics that are relevant and straightforward. This series will be a valuable tool in the local church.
Dennis "Tiger" McLuen, Executive Director,
Youth Leadership

My ministry takes me to the lost kids in our nation's cities where youth games and activities are often irrelevant and plain Bible knowledge for the sake of learning is unattractive. Young people need the information necessary to make wise decisions related to everyday problems. *YouthBuilders* will help many young people integrate their faith into everyday life, which after all is our goal as youth workers.
Miles McPherson, President, Project Intercept

Jim Burns's passion for teens, youth workers and parents of teens is evident in the *YouthBuilders Group Bible Studies*. He has a gift of presenting biblical truths on a

level teens will fully understand, and youth workers and parents can easily communicate.
Al Menconi, President, Al Menconi Ministries

Youth ministry curriculum is often directed to only one spoke of the wheel of youth ministry—the adolescent. Not so with this material! Jim has enlarged the education circle, including information for the adolescent, the parent and the youth worker. *YouthBuilders Group Bible Studies* is youth and family ministry-oriented material at its best.
Helen Musick, Instructor of Youth Ministry,
Asbury Seminary

Finally, a Bible study that has it all! It's action-packed, practical and biblical; but that's only the beginning. *YouthBuilders* involves students in the Scriptures. It's relational, interactive and leads kids toward lifestyle changes. The unique aspect is a page for parents, something that's usually missing from adolescent curriculum. Jim Burns has outdone himself. This isn't a home run—it's a grand slam!
Dr. David Olshine, Director of Youth Ministries,
Columbia International University

Here is a thoughtful and relevant curriculum designed to meet the needs of youth workers, parents and students. It's creative, interactive and biblical—and with Jim Burns's name on it, you know you're getting a quality resource.
Laurie Polich, Youth Director,
First Presbyterian Church of Berkeley

In 10 years of youth ministry I've never used a curriculum because I've never found anything that actively involves students in the learning process, speaks to young people where they are and challenges them with biblical truth—I'll use this! *YouthBuilders Group Bible Studies* is a complete curriculum that is helpful to parents, youth leaders and, most importantly, today's youth.

Glenn Schroeder, Youth and Young Adult Ministries, Vineyard Christian Fellowship, Anaheim

This new material by Jim Burns represents a vitality in curriculum and, I believe, a more mature and faithful direction. *YouthBuilders Group Bible Studies* challenges youth by teaching them how to make decisions rather than telling them what decisions to make. Each session offers teaching concepts, presents options and asks for a decision. I believe it's healthy, the way Christ taught and represents the abilities, personhood and faithfulness of youth. I give it an A+!

J. David Stone, President, Stone & Associates

Jim Burns has done it again! This is a practical, timely and reality-based resource for equipping teens to live life in the fast-paced, pressure-packed adolescent world of the '90s. A very refreshing creative oasis in the curriculum desert!

Rich Van Pelt, President, Alongside Ministries

YouthBuilders Group Bible Studies is a tremendous new set of resources for reaching students. Jim has his finger on the pulse of youth today. He understands their mind-sets, and has prepared these studies in a way that will capture their attention and lead to greater maturity in Christ. I heartily recommend these studies.

Rick Warren, Senior Pastor, Saddleback Valley Community Church

CONTENTS

THANKS AND THANKS AGAIN!

This project is definitely a team effort. First of all, thank you to Cathy, Christy, Rebecca and Heidi Burns, the women of my life.

Thank you to Jill Corey, my incredible assistant and longtime friend.

Thank you to Doug Webster for your outstanding job as executive director of the National Institute of Youth Ministry (NIYM).

Thank you to the NIYM staff in San Clemente: Gary Lenhart, Russ Cline, Laurie Pilz, Luchi Bierbower, Dean Bruns and Larry Acosta.

Thank you to our 100-plus associate trainers who have been my coworkers, friends and sacrificial guinea pigs.

Thank you to Kyle Duncan, Bill Greig III and Jean Daly for convincing me that Gospel Light is a great publisher that deeply believes in the mission to reach young people. I believe!

Thank you to the Youth Specialties world. Tic, Mike and Wayne, so many years ago, you brought on a wet-behind-the-ears youth worker with hair and taught me most everything I know about youth work today.

Thank you to the hundreds of donors, supporters and friends of NIYM. You are helping create an international grassroots movement that is helping young people make positive decisions that will affect them for the rest of their lives.

"Where there is no counsel, the people fall; But in the multitude of counselors there is safety"
(Proverbs 11:14, *NKJV*).

Jim Burns
San Clemente, CA

DEDICATION

To Dr. Mark Hughes:
Thank you, Mark, for your friendship.
Thank you for your fun and free spirit.
Thank you for your servant's heart.
Thank you for your support and encouragement to the National Institute of Youth Ministry and me.
Jesus was the Great Physician and Healer. Thank you for following in His steps.

YOUTHBUILDERS GROUP BIBLE STUDIES

It's Relational—Students learn best when they talk—not when you talk. There is always a get acquainted section in the Warm Up. All the experiences are based on building community in your group.

It's Biblical—With no apologies, this series in unashamedly Christian. Every session has a practical, relevant Bible study.

It's Experiential—Studies show that young people retain up to 85 percent of the material when they are *involved* in action-oriented, experiential learning. The sessions use roleplays, discussion starters, case studies, graphs and other experiential, educational methods. *We believe it's a sin to bore a young person with the gospel.*

It's Interactive—This study is geared to get students feeling comfortable with sharing ideas and interacting with peers and leaders.

It's Easy to Follow—The sessions have been prepared by Jim Burns to allow the leader to pick up the material and use it. There is little preparation time on your part. Jim did the work for you.

It's Adaptable—You can pick and choose from several topics or go straight through the material as a whole study.

It's Age Appropriate—In the "Team Effort" section, one group experience relates best to junior high students while the other works better with high school students. Look at both to determine which option is best for your group.

It's Parent Oriented—The Parent Page helps you to do youth ministry at its finest. Christian education should take place in the home as well as in the church. The Parent Page is your chance to come alongside the parents and help them have a good discussion with their kids.

It's Proven—This material was not written by someone in an ivory tower. It was written for young people and has already been used with them. They love it.

HOW TO USE THIS STUDY

The 12 sessions are divided into three stand-alone units. Each unit has four sessions. You may choose to teach all 12 sessions consecutively. Or you may use only one unit. Or you may present individual sessions. You know your group best so you choose.

Each of the 12 sessions is divided into five sections.

Warm Up—Young people will stay in your youth group if they feel comfortable and make friends in the group. This section is designed for you and the students to get to know each other better. These activities are filled with history-giving and affirming questions and experiences.

Team Effort—Following the model of Jesus, the Master Teacher, these activities engage young people in the session. Stories, group situations, surveys and more bring the session to the students. There is an option for junior high/middle school students and one for high school students.

In the Word—Most young people are biblically illiterate. These Bible studies present the Word of God and encourage students to see the relevance of the Scriptures to their lives.

Things to Think About—Young people need the opportunity to really think through the issues at hand. These discussion starters get students talking about the subject and interacting on important issues.

Parent Page—A youth worker can only do so much. Reproduce this page and get it into the hands of parents. This tool allows quality parent/teen communication that really brings the session home.

THE BIBLE *TUCK-IN*™

It's a tear-out sheet you fold and place in your Bible, containing the essentials you'll need for teaching your group.

HERE'S HOW TO USE IT:

To prepare for the session, first study the session. Tear out the Bible *Tuck-In*™ and personalize it by making notes. Fold the Bible *Tuck-In*™ in half on the dotted line. Slip it into your Bible for easy reference throughout the session. The Key Verse, Biblical Basis and Big Idea at the beginning of the Bible *Tuck-In*™ will help you keep the session on track. With the Bible *Tuck-In*™ your students will see that your teaching comes from the Bible and won't be distracted by a leader's guide.

Unit I

THE BEGINNINGS

LEADER'S PEP TALK

When I started this project on the life of Christ, I had no idea of the great impact it would have on me personally. Writing and teaching these studies on the life and events of Jesus Christ is one of the most challenging and wonderful experiences in my Christian life. While once again studying some of the major events in the life of Jesus, I am reminded of the unconditional and sacrificial love of God.

I love the old Russian proverb that says, "He who has this disease called Jesus Christ will never be cured." I am convinced that if you seriously study the life of Jesus you will never be the same. An encounter with Jesus Christ makes us different. Sometimes it makes us uncomfortable, revealing to us lives that have grown stagnant, and other times it inspires us or gives us hope.

Recently I sat on the beach and watched a baby play in the sand. The little boy crawled around in the sand putting shells, along with anything else he could find, in his mouth. Eventually he wiggled out of his already wet diaper and played the rest of the afternoon innocently. Like every child, he was so vulnerable and totally dependent on his parents' care. And then it hit me. God did that for me! God in the form of a vulnerable baby came into the world so that humankind would have the opportunity to live. He could have done it through marching armies or spectacular displays of miraculous power, but instead He chose to become a helpless little baby, humble and dependent on His own mother.

God's love is incredible. The all-powerful God of the universe became a baby to incarnate His life on earth. He was willing to follow the ritual of the day and be baptized by His cousin John. He was willing to withstand 40 days of temptation in order for the plan of redemption to eventually be accomplished. Studying the life of Christ is being aware of the insanely generous love of God.

My prayer for you and your students is that as you examine these incredible occurrences in the life of Jesus, you will catch a greater glimpse of the depth of His love and the strength of His commitment to you. My hope is that you fall more in love with this God/Man who humbled Himself in the form of a man and then suffered and died in order that we might be set free.

"Therefore God exalted him to the highest place and gave him the name that is above every name, that at the name of Jesus every knee should bow, in heaven and on earth and under the earth, and every tongue confess that Jesus Christ is Lord, to the glory of God the Father" (Philippians 2:9-11).

"You will know the truth, and the truth will set you free" (John 8:32).

Let's make it our prayer that as we tell the stories of Jesus the students in your group will not just intellectualize the life of Christ but rather would be inspired toward deeper commitments as they experience Jesus anew.

THE BIRTH OF JESUS CHRIST

Key Verses

"And there were shepherds living out in the fields nearby, keeping watch over their flocks at night. An angel of the Lord appeared to them, and the glory of the Lord shone around them, and they were terrified. But the angel said to them, 'Do not be afraid. I bring you good news of great joy that will be for all the people. Today in the town of David a Savior has been born to you; he is Christ the Lord.'"
Luke 2:8-11

Biblical Basis

Isaiah 7:14; 9:2,6;
Micah 5:2;
Matthew 1:18-25; 2:1-12;
Luke 2:1-20;
John 3:17; 7:42

The Big Idea

The birth of Jesus Christ was a supernatural event foretold by Old Testament prophecies. His birth shows God's love for our world and reconciles our relationships with God.

Aims of This Session

During this session you will guide students to:
• Examine the important event of the birth of Christ;
• Discover how the birth of Christ is relevant to our Christian faith;
• Implement a response to the Christ child.

Warm Up

The Baby Relay—
A game to get to know one another better.

Team Effort— Junior High/ Middle School

Wise Ones for a Day!—
An activity to give gifts to the Christ child.

Team Effort— High School

The Mary and Joseph Role-Play—
A look at the events concerning the conception of Jesus.

In the Word

The Birth of Jesus—
A Bible study of the events and prophecies concerning the birth of Jesus.

Things to Think About (optional)

Questions to get teens thinking and talking about the relevance of Christ's birth in today's world.

Parent Page

A tool to get the session into the home and allow parents and teens to discuss the significance of Christ's birth to family members.

LEADER'S DEVOTIONAL

"The people walking in darkness have seen a great light; on those living in the land of the shadow of death a light has dawned. For to us a child is born, to us a son is given, and the government will be on his shoulders. And he will be called Wonderful Counselor, Mighty God, Everlasting Father, Prince of Peace" (Isaiah 9:2,6).

Have you ever witnessed the wonderful, amazing process of a baby being born? When Krista gave birth to our first daughter, Janae, I responded with a mouth wide open with amazement and awe. Three years later when our second daughter, Ellie, was born, a spontaneous flow of tears flooded my eyes. Both Janae's and Ellie's births touched undiscovered areas of tenderness in my heart. I believe everyone who experiences the birth of a baby comes away with a new and refreshing perspective on life.

Awe. Amazement. Tenderness. The miraculous birth of a child makes us different people. And so it is with the birth of Jesus Christ, the most miraculous birth of all. Jesus' coming into this world is surrounded by amazing miracles: His coming birth foretold hundreds of years before; the Holy Spirit coming upon a young, courageous teenager named Mary; the amazing birth of His cousin John to a barren woman; the long journey of wise men following a bright and bold star; the startling, glorious appearance of thousands of singing angels praising God before a band of simple shepherds; and the simple, humble, tender birth of the innocent Christ child.

The birth of Christ is a story that never gets old. It's a story that needs to be told and retold, experienced and lived in our hearts every day. Sure, everyone gets bombarded with the Yuletide Madison Avenue merchandising and materialistic media blitz, but nothing can dim or dampen the light of hope found in Jesus' coming to earth.

Though the students you work with may say they've heard the story a thousand times before, you can renew their fascination and appreciation for the birth of Christ by allowing the tenderness of His birth to touch your heart. Maybe it's time to teach this lesson in the maternity ward of a local hospital! Watching an innocent, newborn baby, your students will be amazed. Experiencing the new life found in Jesus Christ for themselves, your students will be transformed. (Written by Joey O'Connor.)

"When we look at the manger we know how He loves us now, you and me, your family, and everybody's family with a tender love. And God loves us with a tender love. That is all that Jesus came to teach us, the tender love of God. 'I have called you by your name, you are Mine.'"
— Mother Teresa

THE BIRTH OF JESUS CHRIST

KEY VERSES

"And there were shepherds living out in the fields nearby, keeping watch over their flocks at night. An angel of the Lord appeared to them, and the glory of the Lord shone around them; and they were terrified. But the angel said to them, 'Do not be afraid. I bring you good news of great joy that will be for all the people. Today in the town of David a Savior has been born to you; he is Christ the Lord.'" Luke 2:8-11

BIBLICAL BASIS

Isaiah 7:14; 9:2,6; Micah 5:2; Matthew 1:18-25; 2:1-12; Luke 2:1-20; John 3:17; 7:42

THE BIG IDEA

The birth of Jesus Christ was a supernatural event foretold by Old Testament prophecies. His birth shows God's love for our world and reconciles our relationships with God.

WARM UP (5-10 MINUTES)
THE BABY RELAY

• Give each student a copy of "The Baby Relay" on page 19 and a pen or pencil.
• Have students complete the page.
  Find someone who has never changed a diaper.

Sign here: ....

Have three people write the name of the hospital and city where they were born.

Name of Hospital .... City

--- Fold ---

Old Testament Prophecy   New Testament Fulfillment

Micah 5:2   Matthew 2:1-6

                                 John 7:42

Isaiah 7:14   Matthew 1:23

B. Mary and Joseph
Read Matthew 1:18-25. If you were Joseph, how would you have reacted when Mary told you she was pregnant?

What factor(s) influenced Joseph and made him change his mind?

C. The Visit of the Wise Men
Read Matthew 2:1-12. What circumstances led to the wise men visiting Jesus in Bethlehem? (See Matthew 2:1-8.)

What did they do when they arrived in Bethlehem? (See Matthew 2:9-12.)

What can you do today that is similar to what the wise men did when they saw Jesus almost 2,000 years ago?

So What?
What specifically is your response to this most incredible event?

THINGS TO THINK ABOUT (OPTIONAL)
• Use the questions on page 23 after or as a part of "In the Word."
1. How do the birth of Jesus and today's celebration of Christmas clash?

2. Why do you think God chose Bethlehem and a manger as the birthplace of the world's Savior?

3. What do you think when you hear the phrase "wise men still seek Him"?

PARENT PAGE
• Distribute page to parents.

Find someone who wants to have more than five children when he or she is married.

Sign here:

Find someone who has visited a maternity ward in a hospital.

Sign here:

Sign here:

Get two other people to sing along with you the first few lines of any song containing the word "baby."

Sign here:

Sign here:

Interview three people and ask them what is the most unique name for a baby that they have ever heard.

Vote for the best one and have the one who suggested the name sign here:

Have someone draw in the space below a portrait of him- or herself as a baby and then autograph the picture.

TEAM EFFORT—JUNIOR HIGH/ MIDDLE SCHOOL (15-20 MINUTES)

WISE ONES FOR A DAY!

• Give students paper and pencils. Have them draw gifts they would give the Christ child.
• Reenact the wise men visiting the baby Jesus in a contemporary setting. Place a picture of a nativity scene or an actual nativity set at the front of the room. Have each person come up to the manger and offer his or her gift to the Christ child. As students offer their gifts, have them explain why they chose the gifts they did. (Examples of the gifts they might

Fold

---

give include: their love, time for Bible reading or prayer, kindness to others, bad habits or influences, money to charity and volunteer work.)

TEAM EFFORT—HIGH SCHOOL (15-20 MINUTES)

THE MARY AND JOSEPH ROLE-PLAY

• Ask four students in your group to read Matthew 1:18-25 and role-play the scene as Mary, Joseph, the angel and a narrator. They can modernize it, use props and enact it in any way they choose.
• Option: Divide students into groups with at least four members in each group. Have each group prepare to enact Matthew 1:18-25. Depending on the size of the group you can have some, or all, of the groups present their versions of the story.
• When the role-play is finished, ask the students these questions:
1. How was this role-play different from what we usually hear about the Christmas story?
2. What was Joseph's first response when Mary told him she was pregnant? What was Joseph's second response to the news?
3. What insights did you get from this role-play?

IN THE WORD (25-30 MINUTES)

THE BIRTH OF JESUS

• Divide students into groups of three or four.
• Give each student a copy of "The Birth of Jesus" on pages 21-23 and a pen or pencil, or display a copy on an overhead projector.
• Have students complete the Bible study.

I. The Event
Read Luke 2:1-20. What part of the story impresses you the most?

List the events in this passage that were supernatural, referring to those events that could not happen unless God arranged them.

II. Looking at the Event
A. The Birth of Jesus Foretold
The Old Testament has a number of prophecies (foretellings of the future) about the birth of the Messiah, Jesus Christ. These prophecies were given to people by God hundreds of years before the birth of Jesus. Let us look at two of these prophecies.

Look up each Scripture and describe the Old Testament prophecy and the New Testament fulfillment in the blank space provided.

WARM UP

THE BABY RELAY

Find someone who has never changed a diaper.

Sign here: ....

Have three people write the name of the hospital and city where they were born.

Name of Hospital	City
....	....
....	....

Find someone who wants to have more than five children when they are married.

Sign here: ....

Find someone who has visited a maternity ward in a hospital.

Sign here: ....

Get two other people to sing along with you the first few lines of any song containing the word "baby."

Sign here: ....

Sign here: ....

Interview three people and ask them what is the most unique name for a baby that they have ever heard.

Vote for the best one and have the one who suggested the name sign here:

....

Have someone draw in the space below a portrait of him- or herself as a baby and then autograph the picture.

 **IN THE WORD**

THE BIRTH OF JESUS

I. The Event

Read Luke 2:1-20. What part of the story impresses you the most?

....

....

List the events in this passage that were supernatural, referring to those events that could not happen unless God arranged them.

....

....

II. Looking at the Event

A. The Birth of Jesus Foretold

The Old Testament has a number of prophecies (foretellings of the future) about the birth of the Messiah, Jesus Christ. These prophecies were given to people by God hundreds of years before the birth of Jesus. Let us look at two of these prophecies.

Look up each Scripture and describe the Old Testament prophecy and the New Testament fulfillment in the blank space provided.

Old Testament Prophecy	New Testament Fulfillment
Micah 5:2	Matthew 2:1-6
....	....
....	....
	John 7:42
....	....
Isaiah 7:14	Matthew 1:23
....	....
....	....

B. Mary and Joseph

Read Matthew 1:18-25.

If you were Joseph, how would you have reacted when Mary told you she was pregnant?

....

....

What factor(s) influenced Joseph and made him change his mind?

....

....

IN THE WORD

THE BIRTH OF
JESUS CHRIST

C.   The Visit of the Wise Men
     Read Matthew 2:1-12

What circumstances led to the wise men visiting Jesus in Bethlehem? (See Matthew 2:1-8.)

....

....

What did they do when they arrived in Bethlehem? (See Matthew 2:9-12.)

....

....

What can you do today that is similar to what the wise men did when they saw Jesus almost 2,000 years ago?

SO WHAT?
What specifically is your response to this most incredible event?

....

....

....

_____

THINGS TO THINK ABOUT

1. How do the birth of Jesus and today's celebration of Christmas clash?

....

....

2. Why do you think God chose Bethlehem and a manger as the birthplace of the world's Savior?

....

....

3. What do you think when you hear the phrase "wise men still seek Him?"

....

....

....

PARENT PAGE

THE BIRTH OF JESUS

According to John 3:17, why was Jesus born on this earth?

....

....

....

On the same day that Jesus was born, an angel appeared to a group of shepherds. Paraphrase what the angel said to them in Luke 2:10,11.

....

....

....

The angel called the baby "Jesus," meaning "The Lord saves." What is unique about a baby being the Savior of the world?

....

....

....

The angel brought news of great joy. How has the birth of Jesus given you joy? Share several reasons for rejoicing that are meaningful to you personally.

....

....

....

What family traditions could you do or have you done that help you worship the baby Jesus?

....

....

....

....

Session 1 "The Birth of Jesus Christ"
Date ....

THE INCARNATION OF GOD

KEY VERSES

"In the beginning was the Word, and the Word was with God, and the Word was God. He was with God in the beginning.

"Through him all things were made; without him nothing was made that has been made. In him was life, and that life was the light of men. The light shines in the darkness, but the darkness has not understood it.

"The Word became flesh and made his dwelling among us. We have seen his glory, the glory of the One and Only, who came from the Father, full of grace and truth." John 1:1-5,14

BIBLICAL BASIS

Genesis 1:1;
Micah 5:4,5;
John 1:1-5,14;
Colossians 1:15-20;
Hebrews 2:17,18

THE BIG IDEA

The Incarnation is the act of God becoming human, whereas Jesus is both fully God and fully human.

AIMS OF THIS SESSION

During this session you will guide students to:
- Examine and understand the incredible truth of the incarnation of God in Jesus Christ;
- Discover how the Incarnation relates to their faith;
- Implement an understanding and commitment to honor God's gift to us in our own walk with Him.

WARM UP

WHAT WOULD YOU DO IF...—

Students decide how they would respond in various situations.

TEAM EFFORT— JUNIOR HIGH/ MIDDLE SCHOOL

THE SCIENCE EXPERIMENT—

An object lesson on the Incarnation.

TEAM EFFORT— HIGH SCHOOL

FULLY GOD—FULLY HUMAN—

Students explore the godly and human attributes of Jesus Christ and relate these to their own lives.

IN THE WORD

THE INCARNATION OF GOD—

A Bible study on the incarnation of Jesus.

THINGS TO THINK ABOUT (OPTIONAL)

Questions to get students thinking and talking about the importance of understanding the concept of the Incarnation.

PARENT PAGE

A tool to get the session into the home and allow parents and young people to discuss how the Incarnation affects their spiritual lives.

LEADER'S DEVOTIONAL

"He will stand and shepherd his flock in the strength of the Lord, in the majesty of the name of the Lord his God. And they will live securely, for then his greatness will reach to the ends of the earth. And he will be their peace" (Micah 5:4,5).

Life is filled with astounding complexities and contradictory realities. For instance, if convenience stores are open 24 hours a day, 365 days a year, why do they have locks on the door? Why do teenage girls tend to go to the restroom in packs of four or five? How is it that some teenage guys spend more time on their hair than some girls? Why do the parents of teenagers set themselves up when they ask their sons or daughters, "What do you think I am…stupid?"

The incarnation of God in the person of Jesus Christ is one of the more complex and difficult concepts to explain to teenagers. To begin with, *it is a mystery.* How could God become fully man, and yet still remain fully God? To simplistically explain it off as a miracle that teenagers must accept won't cut it for most teenagers. Teenagers want to investigate complex issues and discover God's truth on their own. In fact, this is something they need to do in order to personalize and internalize their faith. Since this world is already a complex place to begin with, the incarnation of God is a truth which can lead young people to explore their faith and seek God at a deeper, more meaningful level.

The simplest explanation of the Incarnation is a changed life. A changed life is evidence to the truth of the Incarnation's mystery. If Jesus Christ has invaded your life with His love and that love is poured out into the young people, the Incarnation will be a reality they see in you. The abstract will be made concrete just as the followers of Christ were amazed to see God at work in their presence. That's why there is such power in building positive relationships with young people. Teenagers want love. They want hope. They want someone to trust. Young people want to believe and reach for someone greater than themselves—Someone like God—but they first need to see that reality in someone's life—someone like you. The incarnation of God is a wonderful mystery and miracle. The best explanation you can give to teenagers about the Incarnation is to allow Jesus to live His incredible life through you. (Written by Joey O'Connor.)

"Whatever may happen, however seemingly inimical it may be to the world's going and those who preside over the world's affairs, the truth of the Incarnation remains intact and inviolate…Christ shows what life really is, and what our true destiny is."
— Malcolm Muggeridge

THE INCARNATION OF GOD

KEY VERSES

"In the beginning was the Word, and the Word was with God, and the Word was God. He was with God in the beginning.

"Through him all things were made; without him nothing was made that has been made. In him was life, and that life was the light of men. The light shines in the darkness, but the darkness has not understood it.

"The Word became flesh and made his dwelling among us. We have seen his glory, the glory of the One and Only, who came from the Father, full of grace and truth." John 1:1-5,14

BIBLICAL BASIS

Genesis 1:1; Micah 5:4,5; John 1:1-5,14; Colossians 1:15-20; Hebrews 2:17,18

THE BIG IDEA

The Incarnation is the act of God becoming human, whereas Jesus is both fully God and fully human.

WARM UP (5-10 MINUTES)

WHAT WOULD YOU DO IF...

- Give a copy of "What Would You Do If..." on page 31 and a pencil or pen to each student.
- Have the students complete the pages on their own.
- Have one or two students for each question share their answers with the whole group.

  The president asked you to speak to the nation?
  Your best friend told you he/she was going to move to another country?
  You could plan the ultimate four-hour date?
  You were given $1 million?
  You could meet anyone in the world?
  You could go anywhere in the world?

---------- Fold ----------

"Incarnation" means and how it is described in Scripture.

Incarnation means "in the flesh." Jesus Christ is the one and only incarnation of God. He is the embodiment of God. Jesus is fully God and fully human. God visited earth in the form of a human being, Jesus.

So that the meaning of this may penetrate your heart, read the passages below and write in your own words what they mean.

John 1:14

Colossians 1:15-20

Hebrews 2:17,18

After reflecting upon these passages, summarize for yourself what the word "incarnation" means.

What makes the Incarnation such an important event to the world?

So WHAT?

Each Christmas we are reminded that God's gift to us is Jesus in the flesh. Your gift to God should be your very life.

What areas of your life do you still need to give to God? Start today!

In your small groups share your answers to the previous question and then pray for one another.

THINGS TO THINK ABOUT (OPTIONAL)

- Use the questions on page 41 after or as a part of "In the Word."
1. Why is the Incarnation inseparable from the birth of Christ?

2. How do you feel knowing Jesus Christ was also present at the time of creation?

3. Where in your world is the Spirit of Christ needed?

PARENT PAGE

- Distribute page to parents.

TEAM EFFORT—JUNIOR HIGH/ MIDDLE SCHOOL

THE SCIENCE EXPERIMENT (15-20 MINUTES)

Materials needed: a clear glass, concentrated drink powder, water

- Take a glass and pour in a concentrated drink powder. Pour in water and stir them together. Point out how the powder and the water have mixed to become one drink.
- Discuss as a group the similarities and differences between this "experiment" and the Incarnation.

TEAM EFFORT—HIGH SCHOOL (15-20 MINUTES)

FULLY GOD—FULLY HUMAN

- Divide students into groups of three or four.
- Give each student a copy of "Fully Human—Fully God" on page 33 and a pen or pencil.
- Have students complete the first part of the page together in their groups.
- Have students complete the second and third parts of the page by themselves.

Jesus Christ is the incarnation of God. This means He is fully God and fully human. As a group, brainstorm which parts of Christ represent His godliness and which parts represent His humanness.

CHRIST

Godly	Human
i.e.: His resurrection	i.e.: His temptation

YOU

List on the "Godly" side areas of your life where Christ is involved. On the "Human" side list areas of your life that need to be given to Christ.

Godly	Human
i.e.: share Christ with my friends	i.e.: my relationship with Mom

OUR WORLD

Where does our world need us to be the incarnated love of God?

Godly	Human
i.e.: pray for believers	i.e.: give to the needy

IN THE WORD (25-30 MINUTES)

THE INCARNATION OF GOD

- Divide students into groups of three or four.
- Give students copies of "The Incarnation of God" on pages 35-37 and a pen or pencil, or display the page on an overhead projector.
- Have students complete the Bible study.

I. The Event

"In the beginning was the Word, and the Word was with God, and the Word was God. He was with God in the beginning.

"Through him all things were made; without him nothing was made that has been made. In Him was life, and that life was the light of men. The light shines in the darkness, but the darkness has not understood it.

"The Word became flesh and made his dwelling among us. We have seen his glory, the glory of the One and Only, who came from the Father, full of grace and truth" (John 1:1-5,14).

"The Word" in the Scripture above represents Jesus. What can we learn about Jesus from this passage?

How does this Scripture relate to the story of the birth of Jesus?

Why is the event recorded in John 1:1-5,14 so important to the Christmas story?

II. Looking at the Event
This Word that creates and sustains the world has become a person!

A. The Creation
Read Genesis 1:1 and John 1:1. What are the similarities between these two passages?

What part did Jesus (the Word) have in the creation of the world, according to John 1:1-3?

B. Who Is Jesus?
Many people get confused when they try to figure out exactly who Jesus really is. Is He God or is He man? He was born of the flesh. Mary gave birth to Him. There was a time and a place. Yet the Bible teaches that He was from the beginning of time. To grasp this truth, you must remember that our finite minds cannot always comprehend the infinite God. However, the best way to understand is to learn what the word

THE INCARNATION OF GOD

WHAT WOULD YOU DO IF...

The president asked you to speak to the nation?

Your best friend told you he/she was going to move to another country?

You could plan the ultimate four-hour date?

You were given $1 million?

You could meet anyone in the world?

You could go anywhere in the world?

FULLY GOD—FULLY HUMAN

Jesus Christ is the incarnation of God. This means He is fully God and fully human. As a group, brainstorm which parts of Christ represent His godliness and which parts represent His humanness.

CHRIST

Godly	Human
i.e.: His resurrection	i.e.: His temptation

YOU

List on the "Godly" side areas of your life where Christ is involved. On the "Human" side list areas of your life that need to be given to Christ.

Godly	Human
i.e.: share Christ with my friends	i.e.: my relationship with Mom

OUR WORLD

Where does our world need us to be the incarnated love of God?

Godly	Human
i.e.:pray for believers	i.e.: give to the needy

⬤N THE WORD

THE INCARNATION OF GOD

I. **The Event**

"In the beginning was the Word, and the Word was with God, and the Word was God.
He was with God in the beginning.

"Through him all things were made; without him nothing was made that has been made.
In Him was life, and that life was the light of men. The light shines in the darkness, but
the darkness has not understood it.

"The Word became flesh and made his dwelling among us. We have seen his glory, the glory
of the One and Only, who came from the Father, full of grace and truth" (John 1:1-5,14).

"The Word" in the Scripture above represents Jesus. What can we learn about Jesus from this passage?

....

....

How does this Scripture relate to the story of the birth of Jesus?

....

....

Why is the event recorded in John 1:1-5,14 so important to the Christmas story?

....

....

II. **Looking at the Event**

This Word that creates and sustains the world has become a person!

A. **The Creation**
Read Genesis 1:1 and John 1:1
What are the similarities between these two passages?

....

....

What part did Jesus (the Word) have in the creation of the world, according to John 1:1-3?

....

....

....

IN THE WORD

B. Who Is Jesus?

Many people get confused when they try to figure out exactly who Jesus really is. Is He God or is He man? He was born of the flesh. Mary gave birth to Him. There was a time and a place. Yet the Bible teaches that He was from the beginning of time. To grasp this truth, you must remember that our finite minds cannot always comprehend the infinite God. However, the best way to understand is to learn what the word "incarnation" means and how it is described in Scripture.

Incarnation means "in the flesh." Jesus Christ is the one and only incarnation of God. He is the embodiment of God. Jesus is fully God and fully human. God visited earth in the form of a human being, Jesus.

So that the meaning of this may penetrate your heart, read the passages below and write in your own words what they mean.

John 1:14

....
....

Colossians 1:15-20

....
....

Hebrews 2:17,18

....
....

After reflecting upon these passages, summarize for yourself what the word "incarnation" means.

....
....
....

What makes the Incarnation such an important event to the world?

....
....
....

So What?

Each Christmas we are reminded that God's gift to us is Jesus in the flesh. Your gift to God should be your very life.

What areas of your life do you still need to give to God? Start today!

....

....

....

In your small groups share your answers to the previous question and then pray for one another.

....

....

*T*HINGS TO THINK ABOUT

1. Why is the Incarnation inseparable from the birth of Christ?

....

....

2. How do you feel knowing Jesus Christ was also present at the time of creation?

....

....

3. Where in your world is the Spirit of Christ needed?

....

....

....

Parent Page

THE INCARNATION AND YOU

Once upon a time there was a colony of ants who were busy doing whatever ants do with their lives. God wanted to tell the ants of His love for them and His eternal home He had prepared for them. What is the very best way for God to communicate to those ants? The only possible way to speak to the ants is to become an ant and speak their language. So He did, and they believed.

The Incarnation represents the ultimate act of God's love. God answered the question "How do you package love?" by using a stable and straw and a tiny Baby.

The baby Jesus, born in a stable and straw, was fully human and fully God.

What makes this act of God a sign of deep love?

....

....

....

Why is it so difficult to comprehend God's unconditional love?

....

....

....

Read Hebrews 2:17,18. How is Jesus able to identity with you?

....

....

....

How can this Scripture help you live your Christian life?

....

....

....

What can you do as a family to live out the incarnation of God in a more direct way?

....

....

....

Session 2 "The Incarnation of God"
Date ....

THE BAPTISM OF JESUS

KEY VERSES

"Then Jesus came from Galilee to the Jordan to be baptized by John. But John tried to deter him, saying 'I need to be baptized by you, and do you come to me?'

"Jesus replied, 'Let it be so now; it is proper for us to do this to fulfill all righteousness.' Then John consented.

"As soon as Jesus was baptized, he went up out of the water. At that moment heaven was opened, and he saw the Spirit of God descending like a dove and lighting on him. And a voice from heaven said, 'This is my Son, whom I love; with him I am well pleased.'" Matthew 3:13-17

BIBLICAL BASIS

Isaiah 11:1,2;
Matthew 3:1-4,13-17;
Mark 1:7,8;
Luke 1:5-25,36,39-45,57-66;
John 1:29-31;
Romans 6:3,4;
2 Peter 3:9;
1 John 1:9

THE BIG IDEA

The baptism of Jesus was a public act of Jesus' submission to the Father and the Father's blessing of His Son.

AIMS OF THIS SESSION

During this session you will guide students to:

• Examine the baptism of Jesus and its surrounding events;

• Discover the importance of the baptism of Jesus and how baptism relates to us;

• Implement a decision to look personally at the significance of our own baptism and make any decisions needed based on our findings.

WARM UP

WOULD YOU RATHER—

Students discover one another's likes and dislikes.

TEAM EFFORT— JUNIOR HIGH/ MIDDLE SCHOOL

A BAPTISM—

An experience and discussion of baptism.

TEAM EFFORT— HIGH SCHOOL

A STARTING OVER CEREMONY—

An understanding of confession, repentance and forgiveness.

IN THE WORD

THE BAPTISM OF JESUS—

A Bible study on Jesus' baptism.

THINGS TO THINK ABOUT (OPTIONAL)

Questions to get students thinking and talking about the significance of baptism in their own lives.

PARENT PAGE

A tool to get the session into the home and allow parents and young people to discuss the importance of baptism.

LEADER'S DEVOTIONAL

"A shoot will come up from the stump of Jesse; from his roots a Branch will bear fruit. The Spirit of the Lord will rest on him—the Spirit of wisdom and of understanding, the Spirit of counsel and of power, the Spirit of knowledge and of the fear of the Lord" (Isaiah 11:1,2).

I've always loved the exciting celebration of watching teenagers "go public" with their faith through the ceremony of baptism. I've had the privilege of baptizing young people shivering in icy pools waiting their turn to be "dunked for Jesus." Other students I've baptized have had it easier—being baptized in a warm, soothing Jacuzzi. Whether it's watching teenagers sliding under the rushing water of a frigid mountain stream at six A.M. or standing on the ocean shore at eleven o'clock at night with flashlights, baptism is a very special event in the life of every Christian.

The baptism of Jesus teaches all of us, youth workers and students alike, the importance of submitting to the will of God. When Jesus was baptized by John, He died to His will and completely submitted Himself to the will of His Father in heaven. Not only did He identify with the human traditions of His day, He defied human nature in its rebellion against God. In His baptism, Jesus stood with mankind in its need for redemption and He stood against the power of sin by abandoning Himself to the power and will of God.

As a youth worker, you have the unique privilege of teaching young people the significance of Christ's baptism. You also can have the special opportunity to plan and prepare meaningful baptism ceremonies that they will remember forever. Baptism is a perfect opportunity for you to dig into students' lives and encourage them to be all that God desires them to be.

Jesus doesn't ask you or teenagers to do anything He wasn't first willing to do Himself. Jesus shows us that not only is submitting to God possible, but by submitting ourselves to God, we also receive the blessing of God. Baptism is a celebration of new life. Only by submitting ourselves to God will we truly experience the celebration He has planned for us. (Written by Joey O'Connor.)

"Example is not the main thing in influencing others. It is the only thing."—Albert Schweitzer

Tear along perforation. Fold and place this Bible *Tuck-In*™ in your Bible for session use.

THE BAPTISM OF JESUS

KEY VERSES

"Then Jesus came from Galilee to the Jordan to be baptized by John. But John tried to deter him, saying 'I need to be baptized by you, and do you come to me?'

"Jesus replied, 'Let it be so now; it is proper for us to do this to fulfill all righteousness.' Then John consented.

"As soon as Jesus was baptized, he went up out of the water. At that moment heaven was opened, and he saw the Spirit of God descending like a dove and lighting on him. And a voice from heaven said 'This is my Son, whom I love; with him I am well pleased.'"
Matthew 3:13-17

BIBLICAL BASIS

Isaiah 11:1,2; Matthew 3:1-4,13-17; Mark 1:7,8; Luke 1:5-25,36,39-45,57-66; John 1:29-31; Romans 6:3,4; 2 Peter 3:9; 1 John 1:9

THE BIG IDEA

The baptism of Jesus was a public act of Jesus' submission to the Father and the Father's blessing of His Son.

WARM UP (5-10 MINUTES)

WOULD YOU RATHER

• Have the students stand and then tell them that they should move to the side of the room you indicate as you read each of the following questions. Give a few seconds for them to respond before moving on to the next question.
Would you rather: (Point to the right as you read the first item in each pair and to the left for the second item.)
  eat candy or eat filet mignon?
  drive a sports car or ride a horse?
  vacation in Hawaii or vacation in Europe?
  date a lot of people or date one person?

Fold

Describe John's physical appearance. (See Matthew 3:4.)

What did John say to the people about Jesus and His baptism? (See Mark 1:7,8.)

B. The Baptism
Since baptism is a sign of repentance of sin, why do you suppose John was reluctant to baptize Jesus? (See Matthew 3:13,14.)

What did John the Baptist say as he saw Jesus coming to be baptized? (See John 1:29-31.)

What is so significant about these words that John the Baptist spoke?

Read Matthew 3:16,17. What miraculous experiences took place at the baptism of Jesus?

What makes this event so significant in the life and ministry of Jesus Christ?

So WHAT?
What does baptism mean to you?

Baptism signifies a new life and a new beginning. What does Romans 6:3,4 say about the new life available in Christ?

Baptism also signifies repentance. Repentance means to turn away from your sins and dedicate yourself to go in God's direction. Repentance is a continual act of turning our lives over to God.

List three areas of your life you would like to turn over to God.

God chose Jesus' baptism to be the symbol of a tremendous change in Jesus' life—the beginning of His public ministry. Take some time today to reflect on your baptism and the significance it has in your life and ministry.

THINGS TO THINK ABOUT (OPTIONAL)
• Use the questions on page 53 after or as a part of "In the Word."
1. How would you feel if you were John baptizing Jesus?

2. Why is baptism so important to the Christian faith?

3. What keeps you from having faith more like that of John the Baptist?

PARENT PAGE
•Distribute page to parents.

learn to surf or learn to play a musical instrument? be a missionary or be an attorney?

TEAM EFFORT—JUNIOR HIGH/
MIDDLE SCHOOL (15-20 Minutes)

A BAPTISM
• The most valuable "hands-on" experience would be for the group members to experience or observe a baptism. Plan part of the meeting around an actual baptism and then discuss the significance and meaning of baptism.
• Option: If witnessing or participating in an actual baptism is not possible, invite your pastor or someone else knowledgeable on the doctrine of baptism to come in and discuss the importance of this experience.

Confession

Repentance

Forgiveness

TEAM EFFORT—HIGH SCHOOL (15-20 Minutes)

A STARTING OVER CEREMONY
• Give each student a copy of "A Starting Over Ceremony" on page 47 and a pen or pencil.
• Read the handout directions to the students and allow them time to write down their responses. As the leader, take a few minutes to assure them of their forgiveness in Christ. Baptism is a beautiful symbol of new life in Christ and the washing away of our sins. **Three elements of importance to baptism are:**

CONFESSION
"If we confess our sins, he is faithful and just and will forgive us our sins and purify us from all unrighteousness" (1 John 1:9).
List those actions, thoughts and words where you have missed the mark with God.

REPENTANCE
"The Lord is not slow in keeping his promise, as some understand slowness. He is patient with you, not wanting anyone to perish, but everyone to come to repentance" (2 Peter 3:9).
This means to turn away from your past sin. Write out what you will do to turn away from the sins you have confessed.

FORGIVENESS
"If we confess our sins, he is faithful and just and will forgive us our sins and purify us from all unrighteousness" (1 John 1:9).

Fold

According to this promise of God, what has taken place through the confession of sin?

Is this forgiveness based on your goodness?

Because of the forgiveness of Christ, in what areas can you start over?

IN THE WORD (25-30 Minutes)

THE BAPTISM OF JESUS
• Divide the students into groups of three or four.
• Give each student a copy of "The Baptism of Jesus" on pages 49-51 and a pen or pencil, or display a copy using an overhead projector.
• Have students complete the Bible study.

I. The Event
"Then Jesus came from Galilee to the Jordan to be baptized by John. But John tried to deter him, saying, 'I need to be baptized by you, and do you come to me?' 'Jesus replied, 'Let it be so now; it is proper for us to do this to fulfill all righteousness.' Then John consented. "As soon as Jesus was baptized, he went up out of the water. At that moment heaven was opened, and he saw the Spirit of God descending like a dove and lighting on him. And a voice from heaven said, 'This is my Son, whom I love; with him I am well pleased'" (Matthew 3:13-17).

Who baptized Jesus?

What did the one who baptized Jesus say about the idea of doing so?

What was Jesus' response?

What is significant about the baptism of Jesus, according to Matthew 3:16,17?

II. Looking at the Event
A. John the Baptist
John the Baptist plays an important part in the life of Christ. He was even Jesus' relative by birth (see Luke 1:36). You will gain a better understanding of who he was by answering the questions below.
Summarize the miraculous events surrounding the birth of John. (See Luke 1:5-25, 39-45, 57-66.)

What was John's God-given task in life? (See Matthew 3:1-3.)

What did John the Baptist preach? (See Matthew 3:2.)

⊤EAM EFFORT

THE
BEGINNINGS

THE
BAPTISM
OF JESUS

A STARTING OVER CEREMONY

Baptism is a beautiful symbol of new life in Christ and the washing away of our sins. Three elements of importance to baptism are:

Confession

Repentance

Forgiveness

Confession

"If we confess our sins, he is faithful and just and will forgive us our sins and purify us from all unrighteousness" (1 John 1:9).

List those actions, thoughts and words where you have missed the mark with God.

....

....

Repentance

"The Lord is not slow in keeping his promise, as some understand slowness. He is patient with you, not wanting anyone to perish, but everyone to come to repentance" (2 Peter 3:9).

This means to turn away from your past sin. Write out what you will do to turn away from the sins you have confessed.

....

....

Forgiveness

"If we confess our sins, he is faithful and just and will forgive us our sins and purify us from all unrighteousness" (1 John 1:9).

According to this promise of God, what has taken place through the confession of sin?

....

....

Is this forgiveness based on your goodness?

....

....

Because of the forgiveness of Christ, in what areas can you start over?

....

....

THE BAPTISM OF JESUS

I. The Event

"Then Jesus came from Galilee to the Jordan to be baptized by John. But John tried to deter him, saying, 'I need to be baptized by you, and do you come to me?'

"Jesus replied, 'Let it be so now; it is proper for us to do this to fulfill all righteousness.' Then John consented.

"As soon as Jesus was baptized, he went up out of the water. At that moment heaven was opened, and he saw the Spirit of God descending like a dove and lighting on him. And a voice from heaven said, 'This is my Son, whom I love; with him I am well pleased'" (Matthew 3:13-17).

Who baptized Jesus?

....

What did the one who baptized Jesus say about the idea of doing so?

....

....

What was Jesus' response?

....

....

What is significant about the baptism of Jesus, according to Matthew 3:16,17?

....

....

II. Looking at the Event

A. John the Baptist

John the Baptist plays an important part in the life of Christ. He was even Jesus' relative by birth (see Luke 1:36). You will gain a better understanding of who he was by answering the questions below.

Summarize the miraculous events surrounding the birth of John. (See Luke 1:5-25, 39-45, 57-66.)

....

What was John's God-given task in life? (See Matthew 3:1-3.)

....

What did John the Baptist preach? (See Matthew 3:2.)

....

IN THE WORD

Describe John's physical appearance. (See Matthew 3:4.)

....

....

What did John say to the people about Jesus and His baptism? (See Mark 1:7,8.)

....

....

B. The Baptism

Since baptism is a sign of repentance of sin, why do you suppose John was reluctant to baptize Jesus? (See Matthew 3:13,14.)

....

....

What did John the Baptist say as he saw Jesus coming to be baptized? (See John 1:29-31.)

....

....

What is so significant about these words that John the Baptist spoke?

....

....

Read Matthew 3:16,17. What miraculous experiences took place at the baptism of Jesus?

....

....

What makes this event so significant in the life and ministry of Jesus Christ?

....

....

So What?

What does baptism mean to you?

....

....

Baptism signifies a new life and a new beginning. What does Romans 6:3,4 say about the new life available in Christ?

....

....

Baptism also signifies repentance. Repentance means to turn away from your sins and dedicate yourself to go in God's direction. Repentance is a continual act of turning our lives over to God.

List three areas of your life you would like to turn over to God.

....

....

....

God chose Jesus' baptism to be the symbol of a tremendous change in Jesus' life the beginning of His public ministry. Take some time today to reflect on your baptism and the significance it has in your life and ministry.

Things to Think About

1. How would you feel if you were John baptizing Jesus?

....

....

....

2. Why is baptism so important to the Christian faith?

....

....

....

3. What keeps you from having faith more like that of John the Baptist?

....

....

....

PARENT PAGE

BAPTISM AND OUR FAMILY

THE BEGINNINGS

THE BAPTISM OF JESUS

My Baptism

Take a few moments for each family member to answer these questions:

What does your baptism mean to you?

....
....
....

Has there ever been a moment(s) in your life where your baptism took on a more significant meaning?

....
....
....

In what areas of your life have you seen God's forgiveness?

....
....
....

Here's how you could support and encourage me at this time in my life.

Session 3 "The Baptism of Jesus"

Date ....

THE TEMPTATION IN THE WILDERNESS

Key Verses

"Then Jesus was led by the Spirit into the desert to be tempted by the devil. After fasting forty days and forty nights, he was hungry. The tempter came to him and said, 'If you are the Son of God, tell these stones to become bread.'

"Jesus answered, 'It is written: "Man does not live on bread alone, but on every word that comes from the mouth of God."'

"Then the devil took him to the holy city and had him stand on the highest point of the temple. 'If you are the Son of God,' he said, 'throw yourself down. For it is written: "He will command his angels concerning you, and they will lift you up in their hands, so that you will not strike your foot against a stone."'

"Jesus answered him, 'It is also written: "Do not put the Lord your God to the test."'

"Again, the devil took him to a very high mountain and showed him all the kingdoms of the world and their splendor. 'All this I will give you,' he said, 'if you will bow down and worship me.'

"Jesus said to him, 'Away from me, Satan! For it is written: "Worship the Lord your God, and serve him only."'

"Then the devil left him, and angels came and attended him." Matthew 4:1-11

Biblical Basis

Psalm 37:4; Matthew 4:1-11; Acts 1:8; Romans 8:28; 1 Corinthians 10:13; Ephesians 6:10-13; Philippians 1:6; 4:19; James 1.5, 4.7,8

The Big Idea

Jesus faced severe temptations and stood firm without compromise. Through God's power, we can overcome temptation.

Aims of This Session

During this session you will guide students to:
- Examine the biblical story of the temptations of Jesus;
- Discover how Christ overcame the temptations of Satan;
- Implement a plan to overcome temptations in their lives.

Warm Up

My Best Day—
Students plan their best day.

Team Effort— Junior High/ Middle School

Top 10 Temptations Facing Teenagers Today—
Students make a list of temptations and how to avoid them.

Team Effort— High School

The Buddy-Buddy System—
An opportunity for students to share with and pray for one another.

In the Word

The Temptation in the Wilderness—
A Bible study on Jesus' resistance to Satan's temptations.

Things to Think About (OPTIONAL)

Questions to get students thinking and talking about dealing with temptation in their own lives.

Parent Page

A tool to get the session into the home and allow parents and young people to discuss how to handle temptation using God's Word.

Leader's Devotional

"Finally, be strong in the Lord and in his mighty power. Put on the full armor of God so that you can take your stand against the devil's schemes. For our struggle is not against flesh and blood, but against the rulers, against the authorities, against the powers of this dark world and against the spiritual forces of evil in the heavenly realms. Therefore put on the full armor of God, so that when the day of evil comes, you may be able to stand your ground, and after you have done everything, to stand" (Ephesians 6:10-13).

One of the most paralyzing accusations Satan can throw at you as a youth worker is, "How can you possibly call yourself a Christian youth worker when you struggle with such thoughts and temptations? How can you expect to help young people become like Christ when you think and do things that bring shame to the cause of Christ? Ha!"

As uncreative as it is, Satan's strategy to discourage and break you down is the same strategy he tried on Jesus. Satan has been there, done that. His lies can penetrate your heart and mind with half-truths, searing accusations and all-out lies. He will do anything to weaken your resolve to follow Jesus and minister to students in need of His grace. I know his ploys all too well. *Been there, done that.*

As a minister to young people and their families, I could become completely overwhelmed if I focused on the failings, inadequacies, sins and temptations I struggle with. For as much as I encourage young people to live radically for God and allow Him to change their lives, I am as quickly dismayed when I see such slow spiritual progress in certain areas of my own life. That's why I unashamedly admit my need for God and throw myself on the grace of Christ, allowing Him to be the Author and Defender of my faith. I am not accountable to Satan. Because of Jesus Christ's blood for my sins, I can humbly and gratefully stand with God as His child.

There's no other way to say it: temptation stinks. As humans, we both love it and hate it. Our sinful natures are drawn to it within a moment's notice. Our spiritual natures abhor and are repulsed by it. If you're discouraged by the temptations in your life, I'm sure Jesus' temptation in the wilderness found in this lesson will give you the perspective you need. Perfection is Christ's work. Progressing in the process God initiated in our lives is our choice and responsibility. God has called you to a Person and a process. It is the journey you are walking with Jesus every day. He has all the grace you need to stand against Satan's sneaky strategies. Jesus knows how to whip Satan. He's been there, done that. (Written by Joey O'Connor.)

"Temptations in the life of faith are not accidents, each temptation is part of a plan, a step in the progress of faith."
— Oswald Chambers

Tear along perforation. Fold and place this Bible Tuck-In™ in your Bible for session use.

SESSION FOUR   BIBLE TUCK-IN ™

THE TEMPTATION IN THE WILDERNESS

KEY VERSES

"Then Jesus was led by the Spirit into the desert to be tempted by the devil. After fasting forty days and forty nights, he was hungry. The tempter came to him and said, 'If you are the Son of God tell these stones to become bread.'

"Jesus answered, 'It is written: "Man does not live on bread alone, but on every word that comes from the mouth of God."'

"Then the devil took him to the holy city and had him stand on the highest point of the temple. 'If you are the Son of God,' he said, 'throw yourself down. For it is written: "He will command his angels concerning you, and they will lift you up in their hands, so that you will not strike your foot against a stone."'

"Jesus answered him, 'It is also written: "Do not put the Lord your God to the test."'

"Again, the devil took him to a very high mountain and showed him all the kingdoms of the world and their splendor. 'All this I will give you,' he said, 'if you will bow down and worship me.'

"Jesus said to him, 'Away from me, Satan! For it is written: "Worship the Lord your God, and serve him only."'

"Then the devil left him, and angels came and attended him." Matthew 4:1-11

BIBLICAL BASIS

Psalm 37:4; Matthew 4:1-11; Acts 1:8; Romans 8:28; 1 Corinthians 10:13; Ephesians 6:10-13; Philippians 1:6; 4:19; James 1:5; 4:7,8

THE BIG IDEA

Jesus faced severe temptations and stood firm without compromise. Through God's power, we can overcome temptation.

WARM UP (5-10 MINUTES)
MY BEST DAY

• Divide students into groups of three or four.

• Have students share with others in their groups what their best days would be like. They can use place, events, people, experiences and their imaginations.

59

Fold

Have you ever put the Lord to a test? If so, what did you learn from the experience?

"Away from me, Satan! For it is written: 'Worship the Lord your God, and serve him only'" (v. 10).

What does this statement mean?

How is this response important in helping you overcome temptation?

How does James 4:7,8 relate to Jesus' statement?

So What?
The Temptation in the Wilderness and You
If you could summarize the temptations in your life with one word it would probably be "compromise." Satan tempted Jesus to compromise His life for selfish power. Jesus showed us we can never defeat evil by compromising, by meeting evil halfway. Everyone struggles with compromise.
Finish this sentence: "The most difficult area for me not to compromise in is...."
What is the best way to combat your temptations?

THINGS TO THINK ABOUT (OPTIONAL)
• Use the questions on page 67 after or as a part of "In the Word."
1. How does it feel to know that Christ was also tempted?

2. What temptations are most common to young people?

3. What makes temptation so tempting?

PARENT PAGE
• Distribute page to parents.

TOP 10 TEMPTATIONS FACING TEENAGERS TODAY (15-20 MINUTES)

- On a chalkboard or using an overhead projector, write two headings: "Top 10 Temptations Facing Teenagers Today" and "Ten Tips for Resisting Temptation."
- Brainstorm with the whole group to list their suggestions.
- Option: Divide students into groups of three or four. Give each group a copy of "Top 10 Temptations Facing Teenagers Today" on page 61 and a pen or pencil and have them brainstorm their suggestions.

TEAM EFFORT—HIGH SCHOOL (15-20 MINUTES)

THE BUDDY-BUDDY SYSTEM

- Break your group into pairs.
- Give each student a copy of "The Buddy-Buddy System" on page 61 and a pen or pencil.
- Have them complete the papers and then exchange them with their "buddies." Ask them to take the papers home and pray for one another. Then have the buddies take a few minutes to pray for one another in class. Encourage them to ask how their "buddies" are doing during the next week or even call each other.

A few areas that tempt me are:

....

I could use encouragement in:

....

Pray for me in these areas:

....

I need to change:

....

IN THE WORD (25-30 MINUTES)

THE TEMPTATION IN THE WILDERNESS

- Divide students into groups of three or four.
- Give each student a copy of "The Temptation in the Wilderness" on pages 63-65 and a pen or pencil, or display a copy using an overhead projector.
- Have students complete the Bible study.

1. The Event

"Then Jesus was led by the Spirit into the desert to be tempted by the devil. After fasting forty days and forty nights, he was hungry. The tempter came to him and said, 'If you are the Son of God, tell these stones to become bread.'

"Jesus answered, 'It is written: "Man does not live on bread alone, but on every word that comes from the mouth of God."'

"Then the devil took him to the holy city and had him stand on the highest point of the temple. 'If you are the Son of God,' he said, 'throw yourself down. For it is written: "He will command his angels concerning you, and they will lift you up in their hands, so that you will not strike your foot against a stone."'

"Jesus answered him, 'It is also written: "Do not put the Lord your God to the test."'

"Again, the devil took him to a very high mountain and showed him all the kingdoms of the world and their splendor. 'All this I will give you,' he said, 'if you will bow down and worship me.'

"Jesus said to him, 'Away from me, Satan! For it is written: "Worship the Lord your God, and serve him only."'

"Then the devil left him, and angels came and attended him" (Matthew 4:1-11).

This extraordinary story is an essential part of Jesus' biography. We must approach this story with a unique reverence because in it Jesus is laying bare His innermost heart and soul. In the wilderness Jesus was alone. No one was with Him while He struggled with Satan's attempts to lure Him into temptation. Why do you suppose Christ went immediately from His baptism to His 40-day experience in the wilderness?

In each exchange that Jesus had with Satan, He quoted from the book of Deuteronomy. We can get a better understanding of each temptation as we discover why Jesus quoted these particular passages. On the chart below, write out what the three different temptations were and how Jesus chose to combat each temptation. Then write out what you think the passage means.

Temptations	Jesus' Response	Meaning

II. Looking at the Event

What is Satan called in Matthew 4:3?

....

1. ....

2. ....

3. ....

The biblical meaning of the word "tempt" is actually more closely related to the idea of being "tested." The wilderness temptation was a true test of Jesus' faith. As we investigate this story, we can find many insights for our own lives as we deal with temptations and testing of our faith.

Let us investigate the three responses listed in the chart above.

"Man does not live on bread alone, but on every word that comes from the mouth of God" (v. 4).

What does this statement mean?

....

How is the response important in helping you overcome temptation?

....

"Do not put the Lord your God to the test" (v. 7).

What does this statement mean?

....

How is this response important in helping you overcome temptation?

....

THE TEMPTATION IN
THE WILDERNESS

 TEAM EFFORT

TOP 10 TEMPTATIONS FACING TEENAGERS TODAY

1. ....
2. ....
3. ....
4. ....
5. ....

TEAM EFFORT

THE BUDDY-BUDDY SYSTEM

Complete the following statements and then exchange it with a "buddy." Take a few minutes to pray for one another. Take time during the week to ask how your buddy is doing or even call each other.

A few areas that tempt me are:

....

....

....

I could use encouragement in:

....

....

....

I need to change:

....

....

....

Pray for me in these areas:

....

....

....

THE TEMPTATION IN THE WILDERNESS

I. The Event

"Then Jesus was led by the Spirit into the desert to be tempted by the devil. After fasting forty days and forty nights, he was hungry. The tempter came to him and said, 'If you are the Son of God, tell these stones to become bread.'

"Jesus answered, 'It is written: "Man does not live on bread alone, but on every word that comes from the mouth of God."'

"Then the devil took him to the holy city and had him stand on the highest point of the temple. 'If you are the Son of God,' he said, 'throw yourself down. For it is written: "He will command his angels concerning you, and they will lift you up in their hands, so that you will not strike your foot against a stone."'

"Jesus answered him, 'It is also written: "Do not put the Lord your God to the test."'

"Again, the devil took him to a very high mountain and showed him all the kingdoms of the world and their splendor. 'All this I will give you,' he said, 'if you will bow down and worship me.'

"Jesus said to him, 'Away from me, Satan! For it is written: "Worship the Lord your God, and serve him only."'

"Then the devil left him, and angels came and attended him" (Matthew 4.1-11).

This extraordinary story is an essential part of Jesus' biography. We must approach this story with a unique reverence because in it Jesus is laying bare His innermost heart and soul. In the wilderness Jesus was alone. No one was with Him while He struggled with Satan's attempts to lure Him into temptation.

Why do you suppose Christ went immediately from His baptism to His 40-day experience in the wilderness?

....

....

In each exchange that Jesus had with Satan, He quoted from the book of Deuteronomy. We can get a better understanding of each temptation as we discover why Jesus quoted these particular passages. On the chart below, write out what the three different temptations were and how Jesus chose to combat each temptation. Then write out what you think the passage means.

	Temptations	Jesus' Response	Meaning
1.			
2.			
3.			

IN THE WORD

II. **Looking at the Event**
What is Satan called in Matthew 4:3?

....

The biblical meaning of the word "tempt" is actually more closely related to the idea of being "tested." The wilderness temptation was a true test of Jesus' faith. As we investigate this story, we can find many insights for our own lives as we deal with temptations and testing of our faith.

Let us investigate the three responses listed in the chart above.

"Man does not live on bread alone, but on every word that comes from the mouth of God" (v. 4).

What does this statement mean?

....

How is the response important in helping you overcome temptation?

....

"Do not put the Lord your God to the test" (v. 7).

What does this statement mean?

....

How is this response important in helping you overcome temptation?

....

Have you ever put the Lord to a test? If so, what did you learn from the experience?

....

"Away from me, Satan! For it is written: 'Worship the Lord your God, and serve him only' " (v. 10).

What does this statement mean?

....

How is this response important in helping you overcome temptation?

....

How does James 4:7,8 relate to Jesus' statement?

....

SO WHAT?

The Temptation in the Wilderness and You

If you could summarize the temptations in your life with one word it would probably be "compromise." Satan tempted Jesus to compromise His life for selfish power. Jesus showed us we can never defeat evil by compromising, by meeting evil halfway. Everyone struggles with "compromise."

Finish this sentence: "The most difficult area for me not to compromise in is...."

....

....

....

What is the best way to combat your temptations?

....

....

....

....

THINGS TO THINK ABOUT

1. How does it feel to know that Christ was also tempted?

....

....

2. What temptations are most common to young people?

....

....

....

3. What makes temptation so tempting?

....

....

....

PARENT PAGE

TEMPTATION

Discuss what you think Paul meant when he wrote:

"No temptation has seized you except what is common to man. And God is faithful; he will not let you be tempted beyond what you can bear. But when you are tempted, he will also provide a way out so that you can stand up under it" (1 Corinthians 10:13).

Jesus used Scripture to respond to Satan's temptations. Here is a list of Scriptures to help you win the fight with temptations. For greatest benefit, memorize these reassuring promises from God. Circle the ones that relate most to each of you. Then have each family member share the Scriptures he or she circled and tell why those verses were chosen.

"Delight yourself in the Lord and he will give you the desires of your heart" (Psalm 37:4).

"But you will receive power when the Holy Spirit comes on you; and you will be my witnesses in Jerusalem, and in all Judea and Samaria, and to the ends of the earth" (Acts 1:8).

"And we know that in all things God works for the good of those who love him, who have been called according to his purpose" (Romans 8:28).

"Being confident of this, that he who began a good work in you will carry it on to completion until the day of Christ Jesus" (Philippians 1:6).

"And my God will meet all your needs according to his glorious riches in Christ Jesus" (Philippians 4:19).

"If any of you lacks wisdom, he should ask God, who gives generously to all without finding fault, and it will be given to him" (James 1:5).

Session 4 "The Temptation in the Wilderness"
Date...

SIGNIFICANT EVENTS

LEADER'S PEP TALK

I almost feel that before we do this next section with our students we should take off our shoes. These four sessions seem like they are holy ground. They give us a glimpse of some of the core events in the life of Jesus. Each session is another key moment in the purpose and ministry of Jesus.

Can I be honest with you? These sessions weren't as fun as some sessions I've had with teens. In fact most of this study has been more theological than what I usually do with students. I kept wanting to almost apologize to them: "Next month we'll study Sex, Drugs and Rock Music." And then it hit me: in this section you and I are placing Truth in the lives of our students. Into a world looking for a spectacular display of power and authority, Jesus enters. He gathers together a ragtag band of followers. How pathetic! He shows up to His greatest event riding on an ass. How ridiculous! His last recorded dinner is in some stuffy upper room where He has a customary meal and actually washes His friends' feet. How boring! Then He is crucified like a common criminal. How humiliating! This is the mundane, not the miraculous. This isn't spectacular, it's, well...ordinary.

Jesus has a habit of entering the ordinary and radically changing it forever. Jesus takes what looks like an ordinary event and makes it an eternal demonstration of love. In these sessions, don't miss the extraordinary in the simple acts of the life of Jesus.

As you teach these sessions to your students, I hope you have some fun. But more than that, I hope you will be encouraged that in these next four events in Jesus' life you are giving your students meat instead of milk shakes. This is pure protein. No one can encounter these events of Jesus and walk away the same.

Thanks for your efforts in working with teens. It has eternal benefits—just ask Jesus.

THE GATHERING OF JESUS' DISCIPLES

KEY VERSES

"As Jesus was walking beside the Sea of Galilee, he saw two brothers, Simon called Peter and his brother Andrew. They were casting a net into the lake, for they were fishermen. 'Come, follow me,' Jesus said, 'and I will make you fishers of men.' At once they left their nets and followed him.

"Going on from there, he saw two other brothers, James son of Zebedee and his brother John. They were in a boat with their father Zebedee, preparing their nets. Jesus called them, and immediately they left the boat and their father and followed him." Matthew 4:18-22

BIBLICAL BASIS

Matthew 4:18-22; 6:25-33;
Luke 5:27-32;
John 12:26

THE BIG IDEA

Jesus commands Christians to follow Him and to put God first in their lives.

AIMS OF THIS SESSION

During this session you will guide students to:
- Examine how Jesus gathered His disciples to follow Him;
- Discover the characteristics of a follower of Jesus Christ;
- Implement a response from the students to follow Jesus just like His disciples did almost 2,000 years ago.

WARM UP

CRAZY OR COURAGEOUS?—

Students vote on various activities.

TEAM EFFORT— JUNIOR HIGH/ MIDDLE SCHOOL

THE INFLUENCE OF JESUS CHRIST—

A story about how Jesus has affected the world.

TEAM EFFORT— HIGH SCHOOL

MODERN-DAY DISCIPLES—

Students choose 12 disciples for today.

IN THE WORD

THE GATHERING OF HIS DISCIPLES—

A Bible study on Jesus' choosing of His disciples.

THINGS TO THINK ABOUT (OPTIONAL)

Questions to get students thinking and talking about the cost of being a disciple of Jesus Christ.

PARENT PAGE

A tool to get the session into the home and allow parents and young people to discuss their family's response to Jesus' call to follow Him.

LEADER'S DEVOTIONAL

"Whoever serves me must follow me; and where I am, my servant also will be. My Father will honor the one who serves me" (John 12:26).

If I was Jesus and I had to pick a bunch of teenagers to follow me and then entrust them to carry my message into the whole world, here's who I probably wouldn't pick: I wouldn't pick any teenager with a bad attitude. Who wants to hang around with a whiner or complainer? I certainly wouldn't choose a flaky or irresponsible teenager. How could I ever get anything done if I couldn't count on my followers? I wouldn't select a teenager who was chronically late for every event. He'd probably miss every miracle I'd ever perform. I also wouldn't pick any teenager who was a loud mouth or who couldn't keep a commitment. What's the use of having followers if they're going to embarrass me? And last of all, I definitely wouldn't pick any teenager who wasn't completely dependable and altogether consistent in every word and action.

But then again, I'm not Jesus.

I'm so grateful that Jesus picked a ragtag bunch of inconsistent, irresponsible, undependable fishermen, tax collectors and an assorted pack of undesirable characters to change this world. You and I would have probably fit in just fine. So would the teenagers we work with. Jesus always has a way of doing things backwards, sideways and upside down in comparison with the way this world usually operates.

This lesson is an exciting chance to rediscover God's incredible love and grace for both you and your students. Because we aren't perfect is precisely why Jesus calls us to follow Him. Your students can experience God's grace and acceptance by understanding that Jesus calls them to follow Him regardless of their weaknesses. By following Jesus, both you and your students can lead the empowered life God calls you to in Jesus Christ. (Written by Joey O'Connor.)

"They were not theologians or political leaders—just ordinary men who became extraordinary under the molding hand of the Master Potter: That makes His selection of them the more wonderful...."
—J. Oswald Sanders

BIBLE *TUCK-IN* ™

THE GATHERING OF JESUS' DISCIPLES

KEY VERSES

"As Jesus was walking beside the Sea of Galilee, he saw two brothers, Simon called Peter and his brother Andrew. They were casting a net into the lake, for they were fishermen. 'Come, follow me,' Jesus said, 'and I will make you fishers of men.' At once they left their nets and followed him.

"Going on from there, he saw two other brothers, James son of Zebedee and his brother John. They were in a boat with their father Zebedee, preparing their nets. Jesus called them, and immediately they left the boat and their father and followed him." Matthew 4:18-22

BIBLICAL BASIS

Matthew 4:18-22; 6:25-33; Luke 5:27-32; John 12:26

THE BIG IDEA

Jesus commands Christians to follow Him and to put God first in their lives.

WARM UP (5-10 Minutes)

CRAZY OR COURAGEOUS?

- Give each student a copy of "Crazy or Courageous?" on page 77 and a pen or pencil.
- Have students complete the quiz.
- Discuss the reasons for their answers if time allows.

Vote on whether or not each idea is crazy, courageous or both.

Crazy	Courageous	Both	
☐	☐	☐	Eating garlic
☐	☐	☐	Standing up for your beliefs
☐	☐	☐	Going on a blind date
☐	☐	☐	Bringing your Bible to school
☐	☐	☐	Being a friend to someone who isn't very popular
☐	☐	☐	Breaking up over the phone
☐	☐	☐	Breaking up in person
☐	☐	☐	Flying a jet with the Blue Angels
☐	☐	☐	Joining a rock band

I. Disciples are willing to put God first in their lives.
   What do you think it means to put God first in your life?

How do the disciples' responses in Matthew 4:20,22 relate to putting God first?

At times we all have trouble keeping God as our number one priority in life. What keeps you from showing God in your heart and in your actions that there is nothing and no one more important than Him?

How can Matthew 6:25-33 help us make the decision to put God first in our lives?

II. Disciples are strongly attracted to Jesus and what He represents.
   Each disciple was willing to leave his old life behind in order to follow Jesus. They were attracted to Jesus' call and believed in His ministry.
   What do you think attracted them to Jesus?

What attracts you to Jesus?

III. Disciples are a diverse group of people.
   The disciples of Jesus were from all walks of life—fishermen, tax collectors, prostitutes, political zealots and even some high-society people. Throughout the ministry of Christ, God seemed to use people who were very different from one another.
   What God-given gifts and talents do you have?

As a disciple of Jesus Christ, how can you use your gifts and talents?

How can Christ use your life to influence others in positive and life-changing directions?

Today Jesus is calling, "Come, follow me, and I will make you fishers of men" (Matthew 4:19). What does that mean to you personally, and what are you willing to do in response to the call?

THINGS TO THINK ABOUT (OPTIONAL)

- Use the questions on page 87 after or as a part of "In the Word."

1. Imagine being a chosen disciple of Jesus during His physical time on earth. What do you think it would have been like to be His disciple during that time in history?

Would you have followed Him? Why, or why not?

2. What causes people to follow Jesus?

3. What makes following Christ so difficult today?

PARENT PAGE

- Distribute page to parents.

Team Effort—Junior High/Middle School

The Influence of Jesus Christ (15-20 Minutes)

- Give each student a copy of "The Influence of Jesus Christ" on page 79.
- Have a student (or an adult) who is a good dramatic reader read "One Solitary Life" to the whole group.
- Discuss the questions that follow the story.

The influence of Jesus has continued, reaching far beyond His first disciples. He is still gathering disciples today and touching our world. Here is a beautiful piece written about the powerful effect of Christ's life.

One Solitary Life

Here is a Man who was born in an obscure village, the Child of a peasant woman. He grew up in another village. He worked in a carpenter shop until He was 30, and then for three years He traveled the country preaching. He never wrote a book. He never held an office. He never owned a home. He never had a family of His own. He never went to college. He never traveled more than two hundred miles from the place where He was born. He never did one of the things that usually accompany greatness. He had no credentials but Himself.

While still a young man, the tide of popular opinion turned against Him. His friends ran away. One of them denied Him. He was turned over to His enemies. He went through the mockery of a trial. He was nailed upon a cross between two thieves. His executioners gambled for the only piece of property He had on earth while He was dying. When He was dead, He was taken down and laid in a borrowed grave through the pity of a friend.

Nineteen centuries have come and gone, and today He is the centerpiece of the human race, and the Leader of the column of progress.

I am far within the mark when I say that all the armies that ever marched, and all the navies that were ever built, and all the parliaments that ever sat, and all the kings that ever reigned, put together have not affected the life of man upon this earth as has that One Solitary Life.—Author Unknown

How do you feel when you read about the effect of Christ's life on our world?

What part did His disciples play in furthering the Christian message?

Team Effort—High School (15-20 Minutes)

Modern-Day Disciples

- Divide students into groups of three or four.
- Give each group one copy of "Modern-Day Disciples" on page 81 and a pen or pencil.
- Have each group complete the sheet and then share its list with the rest of the class.

Design a group of modern-day disciples. Imagine that Jesus comes back to earth to choose 12 modern-day disciples. Who would He choose and why? He has asked your group to help Him by providing a list of "The Top 12

- Telling your mom that her cooking stinks
- Running a marathon race
- Holding a rattlesnake
- Following Jesus no matter what the cost

□ □ □   □ □ □   □ □ □

Disciples." Be ready to explain why you would choose these men and women.

1. ___   7. ___
2. ___   8. ___
3. ___   9. ___
4. ___   10. ___
5. ___   11. ___
6. ___   12. ___

- Have students complete the Bible study.

In The Word (25-30 Minutes)

The Gathering of His Disciples

- Divide students into groups of three or four.
- Give each student a copy of "The Gathering of His Disciples" on pages 83-85 and a pen or pencil, or display a copy on an overhead projector.

I. The Event

"As Jesus was walking beside the Sea of Galilee, he saw two brothers, Simon called Peter and his brother Andrew. They were casting a net into the lake, for they were fishermen. 'Come, follow me,' Jesus said, 'and I will make you fishers of men.' At once they left their nets and followed him. Going on from there, he saw two other brothers, James the son of Zebedee and his brother John. They were in a boat with their father Zebedee, preparing their nets. Jesus called them, and immediately they left the boat and their father and followed him" (Matthew 4:18-22).

What did Jesus say to Peter and Andrew when He invited them to be His disciples? (See v. 19)

What did James and John do in response to the call of Jesus? (See v. 22.)

II. Looking at the Event

It is important to note that Jesus' phrase "follow me" was a known one; it implied that He was calling them to be permanent disciples. If the disciples followed Jesus, they had to give up their professions, their homes, and at times even their families. This call did not come on the first chance meeting with Jesus. He had probably developed a relationship with His disciples before He called them to follow Him.

What is the significance of Jesus' call recorded in Matthew 4:19?

What did the disciples sacrifice in order to follow Jesus?

Read Luke 5:27-32. What can you learn about Jesus from this passage?

So What?

As a child of God you are also a disciple and follower of Jesus Christ. There are three characteristics of Jesus' disciples that remain true today:

WARM UP

CRAZY OR COURAGEOUS?[1]

Vote on whether or not each idea is crazy, courageous or both.

Crazy	Courageous	Both	
❑	❑	❑	Eating garlic
❑	❑	❑	Standing up for your beliefs
❑	❑	❑	Going on a blind date
❑	❑	❑	Bringing your Bible to school
❑	❑	❑	Being a friend to someone who isn't very popular
❑	❑	❑	Breaking up over the phone
❑	❑	❑	Breaking up in person
❑	❑	❑	Flying a jet with the Blue Angels
❑	❑	❑	Joining a rock band
❑	❑	❑	Telling your mom that her cooking stinks
❑	❑	❑	Running a marathon race
❑	❑	❑	Holding a rattlesnake
❑	❑	❑	Following Jesus no matter what the cost

Note:

1. Adapted from an idea by Doug Fields, Saddleback Valley Community Church, Mission Viejo, Calif.

TEAM EFFORT

THE INFLUENCE OF JESUS CHRIST

The influence of Jesus has continued, reaching far beyond His first disciples. He is still gathering disciples today and touching our world. Here is a beautiful piece written about the powerful effect of Christ's life.

One Solitary Life

Here is a Man who was born in an obscure village, the Child of a peasant woman. He grew up in another village. He worked in a carpenter shop until He was 30, and then for three years He traveled the country preaching. He never wrote a book. He never held an office. He never owned a home. He never had a family of His own. He never went to college. He never traveled more than two hundred miles from the place where He was born. He never did one of the things that usually accompany greatness. He had no credentials but Himself.

While still a young man, the tide of popular opinion turned against Him. His friends ran away. One of them denied Him. He was turned over to His enemies. He went through the mockery of a trial. He was nailed upon a cross between two thieves. His executioners gambled for the only piece of property He had on earth while He was dying. When He was dead, He was taken down and laid in a borrowed grave through the pity of a friend.

Nineteen centuries have come and gone, and today He is the centerpiece of the human race, and the Leader of the column of progress.

I am far within the mark when I say that all the armies that ever marched, and all the navies that were ever built, and all the parliaments that ever sat, and all the kings that ever reigned, put together have not affected the life of man upon this earth as has that One Solitary Life.—Author Unknown

How do you feel when you read about the effect of Christ's life on our world?

....

....

....

What part did His disciples play in furthering the Christian message?

....

....

....

THE GATHERING OF
JESUS' DISCIPLES

MODERN-DAY DISCIPLES

Design a group of modern-day disciples. Imagine that Jesus comes back to earth to choose 12 modern-day disciples. Who would He choose and why? He has asked your group to help Him by providing a list of "The Top 12 Disciples." Be ready to explain why you would choose these men or women.

1. ....
2. ....
3. ....
4. ....
5. ....
6. ....

7. ....
8. ....
9. ....
10. ....
11. ....
12. ....

 **N THE WORD**

THE GATHERING OF HIS DISCIPLES

I.   The Event

"As Jesus was walking beside the Sea of Galilee, he saw two brothers, Simon called Peter and his brother Andrew. They were casting a net into the lake, for they were fishermen. 'Come, follow me,' Jesus said, 'and I will make you fishers of men.' At once they left their nets and followed him.

"Going on from there, he saw two other brothers, James the son of Zebedee and his brother John. They were in a boat with their father Zebedee, preparing their nets. Jesus called them, and immediately they left the boat and their father and followed him" (Matthew 4:18-22).

What did Jesus say to Peter and Andrew when He invited them to be His disciples? (See v. 19.)

....

What did James and John do in response to the call of Jesus. (See v. 22.)

....

II.   Looking at the Event

It is important to note that Jesus' phrase "follow me" was a known one; it implied that He was calling them to be permanent disciples. If the disciples followed Jesus, they had to give up their professions, their homes, and at times, even their families. This call did not come on the first chance meeting with Jesus. He had probably developed a relationship with His disciples before He called them to follow Him.

What is the significance of Jesus' call recorded in Matthew 4:19?

....

What did the disciples sacrifice in order to follow Jesus?

....

Read Luke 5:27-32. What can you learn about Jesus from this passage?

....

....

SO WHAT?

As a child of God you are also a disciple and follower of Jesus Christ. There are three characteristics of Jesus' disciples that remain true today:

I.   Disciples are willing to put God first in their lives.
What do you think it means to put God first in your life?

....

....

IN THE WORD

How do the disciples' responses in Matthew 4:20,22 relate to putting God first?

....

....

At times we all have trouble keeping God as our number one priority in life. What keeps you from showing God in your heart and in your actions that there is nothing and no one more important than Him?

....

....

How can Matthew 6:25-33 help us make the decision to put God first in our lives?

....

....

II.   **Disciples are strongly attracted to Jesus and what He represents.**
      Each disciple was willing to leave his old life behind in order to follow Jesus. They were attracted to Jesus' call and believed in His ministry.
      What do you think attracted them to Jesus?

....

....

What attracts you to Jesus?

....

....

III. **Disciples are a diverse group of people.**
      The disciples of Jesus were from all walks of life—fishermen, tax collectors, prostitutes, political zealots and even some high-society people. Throughout the ministry of Christ, God seemed to use people who were very different from one another.
      What God-given gifts and talents do you have?

....

....

As a disciple of Jesus Christ, how can you use your gifts and talents?

....

....

How can Christ use your life to influence others in positive and life-changing directions?

....

....

Today Jesus is calling, "Come, follow me, and I will make you fishers of men" (Matthew 4:19). What does that mean to you personally, and what are you willing to do in response to the call?

....

THINGS TO THINK ABOUT

1. Imagine being a chosen disciple of Jesus during His physical time on earth. What do you think it would have been like to be His disciple during that time in history?

....

....

....

Would you have followed Him? Why, or why not?

....

....

....

2. What causes people to follow Jesus?

....

....

....

3. What makes following Christ so difficult today?

....

....

....

THE GATHERING OF JESUS' DISCIPLES

 PARENT PAGE

FOLLOW ME

"'Come, follow me,' Jesus said, 'and I will make you fishers of men.' At once they left their nets and followed him" (Matthew 4:19,20).

How has your family responded to Jesus' command, "Follow me"?

Here's what we have done	Improvement needed
....	....
....	....
....	....
....	....
....	....

Complete these sentences:

When it comes to putting God first in my life, I... ....

....

As disciples of Jesus, one day I'd like to see our family... ....

....

Here's how you could help me be a more effective follower of Jesus... ....

....

....

The first time I felt God's call to follow Him in my life was... (If you've never sensed God's call to follow Him, then share that also.)

....

....

....

Now take a few minutes to pray for one another.

Session 5 "The Gathering of His Disciples"

Date ....

THE TRIUMPHAL ENTRY

KEY VERSES

"When he came near the place where the road goes down the Mount of Olives, the whole crowd of disciples began joyfully to praise God in loud voices for all the miracles they had seen:

"'Blessed is the king who comes in the name of the Lord!'

"'Peace in heaven and glory in the highest!'" Luke 19:37-39

BIBLICAL BASIS

Psalm 92:12-14; 118:25;
Isaiah 1:10,15,16;
Zechariah 9:9,
Matthew 21:1-7,9;
Mark 11:8-10; 15:13,14;
Luke 19:28-40

THE BIG IDEA

The triumphal entry of Jesus is the recognition of His Kingship. Our response to Christ the King should be praise.

AIMS OF THIS SESSION

During this session you will guide students to:

- Examine the events and responses surrounding what is commonly called Palm Sunday;
- Discover what their responses to Christ the King should be;
- Implement an active response to Christ the King.

WARM UP

REALLY DUMB STUDENT CHEERING SECTIONS—

Students develop cheers of their own.

TEAM EFFORT— JUNIOR HIGH/ MIDDLE SCHOOL

WELCOME TO EARTH—

Students plan a welcoming party for Jesus.

TEAM EFFORT— HIGH SCHOOL

PRAISE-A-THON—

Students plan a time of worship and praise.

IN THE WORD

THE TRIUMPHAL ENTRY—

A Bible study on the events and emotions surrounding Jesus' triumphal entry into Jerusalem.

THINGS TO THINK ABOUT (OPTIONAL)

Questions to get students thinking and talking about the significance of Palm Sunday.

PARENT PAGE

A tool to get the session into the home and allow parents and young people to praise God together.

LEADER'S DEVOTIONAL

"Hear the word of the Lord, you rulers of Sodom; listen to the law of our God, you people of Gomorrah! When you spread out your hands in prayer, I will hide my eyes from you; even if you offer many prayers, I will not listen. Your hands are full of blood; wash and make yourselves clean. Take your evil deeds out of my sight! Stop doing wrong" (Isaiah 1:10,15,16).

Youth ministry, like life in general, is a unique and often wild mix of triumph and tragedy. As I look back on 10 years of youth ministry experience, I can vividly remember numerous triumphant highlights. Going on countless snow ski, water-ski, rock climbing and mission trips with every sort of teenager imaginable. Praying with students to receive Christ into their hearts for the very first time. Endless one-on-one conversations with young people about what God is doing in their lives. Moments filled with hilarious laughter and spontaneous water fights during long, hot car rides. Times of singing quiet worship songs by warm candlelight.

When Jesus entered Jerusalem on a young colt and was received by thousands of eager, excited people praising His name, perhaps He reflected on the special memories He shared with His disciples. Like the time His disciples came rushing back and exclaimed how they had cast out demons in His name. Or the time when Peter, James and John saw Jesus radiating all of God's glory during His transfiguration. Or maybe the time when the disciples' nets were so full with fish that their heavy nets almost broke.

Jesus' triumphal entry into Jerusalem reminds us of the praise He deserves in our lives. Yes, there were plenty of setbacks, disappointments and discouraging times that Jesus and His disciples faced as people rejected His message. However, for those quick, few moments as Jesus came into Jerusalem on that dusty road, He certainly received the true praise and honor He deserved.

Why not take some time to reflect on the triumphs God has given you in your life and ministry? Why not praise Jesus for the triumphs He has worked in your life? This lesson is a great opportunity for you and your students to deepen your commitments to reflect on and praise Jesus for His triumphant entry into your lives. (Written by Joey O'Connor.)

"Jesus did not come to change Israel's politics. He came to change men's hearts. When He rode into Jerusalem, Jesus presented Himself as a humble king, not a violent conqueror."
— Warren Wiersbe

THE TRIUMPHAL ENTRY

KEY VERSES

"When he came near the place where the road goes down the Mount of Olives, the whole crowd of disciples began joyfully to praise God in loud voices for all the miracles they had seen

"'Blessed is the king who comes in the name of the Lord!'

"'Peace in heaven and glory in the highest!'" Luke 19:37-39

BIBLICAL BASIS

Psalm 92:12-14; 118:25; Isaiah 1:10,15,16; Zechariah 9:9; Matthew 21:1-7,9; Mark 11:8-10; 15:13,14; Luke 19:28-40

THE BIG IDEA

The triumphal entry of Jesus is the recognition of His Kingship. Our response to Christ the King should be praise.

 WARM UP (5-10 Minutes)

REALLY DUMB STUDENT CHEERING SECTIONS

• Display a copy of the cartoon on page 95.

• As a group, brainstorm other ideas for really dumb student cheering sections.

• Option: Have small groups develop "dumb cheers" and then share them with the whole group.

TEAM EFFORT—JUNIOR HIGH/ MIDDLE SCHOOL (15-20 Minutes)

WELCOME TO EARTH

• Divide students into groups of three or four.

• Give each group a piece of paper and a pen or pencil. Tell the students, "You have just been given a few minutes notice to plan a party for Jesus. He is going to visit your church today. What ingredients and experiences would you include in this special visit?"

THINGS TO THINK ABOUT (OPTIONAL)

• Use the questions on page 99 after or as a part of "In the Word."

1. What do you think Jesus was feeling during His entry into Jerusalem?

2. Why did the crowd respond to Christ in such a positive manner on Palm Sunday?

3. How does it feel to see Christ praised on Sunday, but know that by Thursday the same crowd was being turned against Him?

PARENT PAGE

• Distribute page to parents.

Fold

PRAISE-A-THON
• Divide students into three groups according to interests and abilities (music, Bible reading and prayer). These groups need not be equal in number. Option: A fourth group of those with artistic ability could be formed to develop posters of praise.
• Provide each group with the materials necessary to accomplish its task (i.e., transparencies or copies of songs, Bibles, paper, pens or pencils and felt-tip pens).
• Tell students, "The purpose of the Triumphal Entry, what many call 'Palm Sunday,' was to worship and praise King Jesus. We are going to work in groups to create a praise and worship atmosphere. These are the group assignments": Prepare several praise and worship songs. Select the songs you want to use and provide copies or transparencies of the words. Select praise from the Scripture. Give each student in your group a Scripture of praise to read. Prepare words of praise to God through prayer. Option: Create posters of praise to place around the the room.

IN THE WORD (25-30 MINUTES)
• Divide students into groups of three or four.
• Give each student a copy of "The Triumphal Entry" on pages 97-99 and a pen or pencil, or display a copy on an overhead projector.
• Have students complete the Bible study.

THE TRIUMPHAL ENTRY

I. The Event

"After Jesus had said this, he went on ahead, going up to Jerusalem. As he approached Bethphage and Bethany at the hill called the Mount of Olives, he sent two of his disciples, saying to them, 'Go to the village ahead of you, and as you enter it, you will find a colt tied there, which no one has ever ridden. Untie it and bring it here. If anyone asks you, "Why are you untying it?" tell him, "The Lord needs it."'

"Those who were sent ahead went and found it just as he had told them. As they were untying the colt, its owners asked them, 'Why are you untying the colt?'

"They replied, 'The Lord needs it.'

"They brought it to Jesus, threw their cloaks on the colt and put Jesus on it. As he went along, people spread their cloaks on the road.

"When he came near the place where the road goes down the Mount of Olives, the whole crowd of disciples began joyfully to praise God in loud voices for all the miracles they had seen:

"'Blessed is the King who comes in the name of the Lord!'

"'Peace in heaven and glory in the highest!'

"Some of the Pharisees in the crowd said to Jesus, 'Teacher, rebuke your disciples!'

"'I tell you,' he replied, 'if they keep quiet, the stones will cry out'" (Luke 19:28-40).

Jesus made His public entry into Jerusalem on a day that we now know as Palm Sunday. It was a day of victory and rejoicing. People in the crowd praised Jesus as He entered Jerusalem. Probably no one realized that in less than a week many of them would also watch Him die on the cross, executed alongside common criminals.

— — — Fold — — —

List the events that took place on the occasion of the triumphal entry of Jesus into Jerusalem.

II. Looking at the Event

Before Jesus was to go into Jerusalem to celebrate the Passover, He asked His disciples to go to the nearby village of Bethphage and get a donkey's colt for Him to ride into the city. He assumed that permission would be given to use the colt. What is the great significance of Jesus riding on the colt into Jerusalem? (See Zechariah 9:9 and Matthew 21:1-7.)

What did the crowds do as Jesus came riding into Jerusalem, according to the Scripture found in Matthew 21:8 and Mark 11:8?

For the Hebrew people the palm was the symbol of beauty and righteousness. It signified the "king" and was always associated with rejoicing as well as triumph and victory. What does Psalm 92:12-14 tell us about the palm?

How does the above Scripture in the Psalms, and the fact that the people placed the branches on the road before Jesus, help us understand how many of the people felt about Jesus?

What did the crowds shout, according to Matthew 21:9 and Mark 11:9,10?

"Hosanna" means "Save now!" and it was the cry for help that a people in distress addressed to their king or their God. How is Psalm 118:25 similar to the pleas of the people honoring Jesus?

SO WHAT?
The Triumphal Entry and You
Imagine yourself in the crowd honoring Jesus as He entered Jerusalem. What thoughts would have been on your mind as you cried out, "Hosanna [save now]... Blessed is he who comes in the name of the Lord" (Matthew 21:9)?

Now imagine yourself a few days later and this time many of the same people who praised and blessed Jesus were shouting, "Crucify him!...Crucify him!" (Mark 15:13,14). What kinds of emotions would you be feeling now?

A few days after the Crucifixion you now begin to hear rumors that Jesus has been raised from the dead. His disciples have seen Him, and more than 500 people also claim to have seen Him. What would you be thinking and feeling?

 ## Warm Up

REALLY DUMB STUDENT CHEERING SECTIONS

As a group, brainstorm other ideas for really dumb student cheering sections.

....

....

_____

....

....

_____

....

....

_____

THE
TRIUMPHAL ENTRY

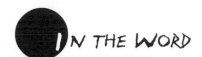

N THE WORD

THE TRIUMPHAL ENTRY

I. **The Event**

"After Jesus had said this, he went on ahead, going up to Jerusalem. As he approached Bethphage and Bethany at the hill called the Mount of Olives, he sent two of his disciples, saying to them, 'Go to the village ahead of you, and as you enter it, you will find a colt tied there, which no one has ever ridden. Untie it and bring it here. If anyone asks you, "Why are you untying it?" tell him, "The Lord needs it."'

"Those who were sent ahead went and found it just as he had told them. As they were untying the colt, its owners asked them, 'Why are you untying the colt?'

"They replied, 'The Lord needs it.'

"They brought it to Jesus, threw their cloaks on the colt and put Jesus on it. As he went along, people spread their cloaks on the road.

"When he came near the place where the road goes down the Mount of Olives, the whole crowd of disciples began joyfully to praise God in loud voices for all the miracles they had seen:

"'Blessed is the King who comes in the name of the Lord!'

"'Peace in heaven and glory in the highest!'

"Some of the Pharisees in the crowd said to Jesus, 'Teacher, rebuke your disciples!'

"'I tell you,' he replied, 'if they keep quiet, the stones will cry out'" (Luke 19:28-40).

Jesus made His public entry into Jerusalem on a day that we now know as Palm Sunday. It was a day of victory and rejoicing. People in the crowd praised Jesus as He entered Jerusalem. Probably no one realized that in less than a week many of them would also watch Him die on the cross, executed alongside common criminals.

List the events that took place on the occasion of the triumphal entry of Jesus into Jerusalem.

....

II. **Looking at the Event**

Before Jesus was to go into Jerusalem to celebrate the Passover, He asked His disciples to go to the nearby village of Bethphage and get a donkey's colt for Him to ride into the city. He assumed that permission would be given to use the colt. What is the great significance of Jesus riding on the colt into Jerusalem? (See Zechariah 9:9 and Matthew 21:1-7.)

....

What did the crowds do as Jesus came riding into Jerusalem, according to the Scripture found in Matthew 21:8 and Mark 11:8?

....

For the Hebrew people the palm was the symbol of beauty and righteousness. It signified the "king" and was always associated with rejoicing as well as triumph and victory. What does Psalm 92:12-14 tell us about the palm?

....

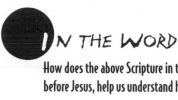

IN THE WORD

How does the above Scripture in the Psalms, and the fact that the people placed the branches on the road before Jesus, help us understand how many of the people felt about Jesus?

....

....

What did the crowds shout, according to Matthew 21:9 and Mark 11:9,10?

....

....

"Hosanna" means "Save now!" and it was the cry for help that a people in distress addressed to their king or their God. How is Psalm 118:25 similar to the pleas of the people honoring Jesus?

....

....

SO WHAT?
THE TRIUMPHAL ENTRY AND YOU

Imagine yourself in the crowd honoring Jesus as He entered Jerusalem. What thoughts would have been on your mind as you cried out, "Hosanna [save now]...Blessed is he who comes in the name of the Lord!" (Matthew 21:9)?

....

....

Now imagine yourself a few days later and this time many of the same people who praised and blessed Jesus were shouting, "Crucify him!...Crucify him!" (Mark 15:13,14). What kinds of emotions would you be feeling now?

....

....

A few days after the Crucifixion you now begin to hear rumors that Jesus has been raised from the dead. His disciples have seen Him, and more than 500 people also claim to have seen Him. What would you be thinking and feeling?

....

....

THINGS TO THINK ABOUT

1. What do you think Jesus was feeling during His entry into Jerusalem?

....

2. Why did the crowd respond to Christ in such a positive manner on Palm Sunday?

....

3. How does it feel to see Christ praised on Sunday, but know that by Thursday the same crowd was being turned against Him?

....

....

PARENT PAGE

The triumphal entry of Jesus was a key event in His life. It is unique because He allowed Himself to be worshiped and called the King.

Take some time and reread this beautiful event in Luke 19:28-40, then write down your own praise to God. Completing the sentences below will help you in your adoration. Now share your words with your family.

I worship God because

....

....

....

I praise God because

....

....

....

I thank God because

....

....

....

He is worthy to be called King and Lord because

....

....

....

Session 6 "The Triumphal Entry"
Date..

THE LAST SUPPER

KEY VERSES

"While they were eating, Jesus took bread, gave thanks and broke it, and gave it to his disciples, saying, 'Take it and eat; this is my body.' Then he took the cup, gave thanks and offered it to them, saying, 'Drink from it, all of you. This is my blood of the covenant, which is poured out for many for the forgiveness of sins. I tell you, I will not drink of this fruit of the vine from now on until that day when I drink it anew with you in my Father's kingdom.'" Matthew 26:26-29

BIBLICAL BASIS

Exodus 12;
Deuteronomy 11:13,14;
Psalm 150:6;
Matthew 26:17-29,47-50; 27:3-5;
Mark 14:12-26;
John 13-16;
James 5:16;
1 John 1:9

THE BIG IDEA

The Last Supper was Jesus' final intimate time with His disciples and an introduction of the act of Communion, or Eucharist.

AIMS OF THIS SESSION

During this session you will guide students to:
• Examine the biblical story of the Last Supper;
• Discover the significance of the disciples' last meal with Jesus and its meaning today;
• Implement an awareness and commitment to make the Communion experience more understandable and meaningful.

WARM UP

UNIQUE FOOD QUESTIONNAIRE—
Students discuss unusual foods.

TEAM EFFORT— JUNIOR HIGH/ MIDDLE SCHOOL

THE COMMUNION EXPERIENCE—
Students partake in the act of Communion.

TEAM EFFORT— HIGH SCHOOL

THE UPPER ROOM EXPERIENCE—
Participation in Communion in a new way.

IN THE WORD

THE LAST SUPPER—
A Bible study on the significance of Passover and the Last Supper.

THINGS TO THINK ABOUT (OPTIONAL)

Questions to get students thinking and talking about the celebration of Communion.

PARENT PAGE

A tool to get the session into the home and allow parents and young people to discuss the heart attitude during Communion.

SIGNIFICANT EVENTS

LEADER'S DEVOTIONAL

"So if you faithfully obey the commands I am giving you today—to love the Lord your God and to serve him with all your heart and with all your soul—then I will send rain on your land in its season, both autumn and spring rains, so that you may gather in your grain, new wine and oil" (Deuteronomy 11:13,14).

Meals have often been a perfect appetizer to help me get to the main course of ministering to a student in need. When I know a teenager is having problems at home or with friends or who has simply dropped out of sight, the easiest, least threatening thing to do is to give him or her a call and ask him or her to go out for a meal. I've never known any teenager to turn down a free meal! Meals provide a comfortable environment for face-to-face, heart-to-heart conversations. Not only does sharing a meal set the table for significant conversation, it's also a wonderful time to develop community and a deeper sense of security and intimacy among friends. Meals have been a key tool of my ministry experience. Almost every high school and college ministry team meeting I've ever had has either begun or ended with a meal…a time to be together…no agenda…just friends…laughing and sharing our lives together.

When Jesus sat with His friends at their final meal together, it was the culmination of many special meals shared together. The Last Supper was Jesus' opportunity to affirm, encourage, pray for and remind His followers of everything He had taught them during the previous three years. It was Jesus' time to show His disciples how to celebrate His life, death and resurrection through the intimate meal of Communion.

The closeness Jesus' disciples experienced with Him at the Last Supper is the same intimacy Jesus wants to share with you. The words of Jesus, particularly in John 13-16, are the words of love He wants to remind you of right now. Jesus calls you to share a meal with Him. It may be Communion or it may simply be inviting His presence around your table tonight. The intimacy and closeness found with Jesus at the Last Supper is not some distant, ancient biblical event. The Living Christ requests the honor of dining with you tonight. (Written by Joey O'Connor.)

"He loves you with more than the love of friendship…He has given you all, and He asks for all in return. The slightest reserve will grieve Him to the heart. He spared not Himself, and how can you spare yourself?"—Hannah Whitall Smith

Tear along perforation. Fold and place this Bible Tuck-In™ in your Bible for session use.

THE LAST SUPPER

KEY VERSES

"While they were eating, Jesus took bread, gave thanks and broke it, and gave it to his disciples, saying, 'Take it and eat; this is my body.' Then he took the cup, gave thanks and offered it to them, saying, 'Drink from it, all of you. This is my blood of the covenant, which is poured out for many for the forgiveness of sins. I tell you, I will not drink of this fruit of the vine from now on until that day when I drink it anew with you in my Father's kingdom.'" Matthew 26:26-29

BIBLICAL BASIS

Exodus 12; Deuteronomy 11:13,14; Psalm 150:6; Matthew 26:17-29,47-50; 27:3-5; Mark 14:12-26; John 13-16; James 5:16; 1 John 1:9

THE BIG IDEA

The Last Supper was Jesus' final intimate time with His disciples and an introduction of the act of Communion, or Eucharist.

WARM UP (5-10 Minutes)

UNIQUE FOOD QUESTIONNAIRE

• Divide students into groups of three or four.
• Give each student a copy of "Unique Food Questionnaire" on page 107 and a pen or pencil, or display a copy using an overhead projector.
• Have students complete the questionnaires in their small groups and then share their answers with the entire group.
What is the weirdest food you have ever eaten? (World's record is dog food sandwich.)
What is the most bizarre combination of foods you have ever eaten? (World's record is peanut butter, carrot and onion sandwich.)
What is the most food you have eaten at one time? (World's record is 12 Taco Bell combination burritos.)
If you were on a desert island and could only eat one meal for a year, what would it be?
What's the worst tasting food you have ever eaten?

Why is Communion, the Eucharist, as special today as it was almost 2,000 years ago?

Now prepare to share this section with the whole group.

So What?

Many of the events of Jesus' life were recorded in the New Testament, but the Last Supper is re-created and remembered regularly by Christians all over the earth. Participating in Communion is an act of remembrance that Jesus Christ's body was broken for you. He died so that you might live. It also means remembering that His blood was shed for you so that your sins would be forgiven. You are righteous before God only because of the broken Body and Blood of Jesus Christ.

When you realize that many thousands of Christians all over the world share with you in Communion, how do you feel?

What makes Communion special for you? If it is not special to you, if it has simply been a ritual, write down your feelings about that.

THINGS TO THINK ABOUT (OPTIONAL)

• Use the questions on page 113 after or as a part of "In the Word."
1. How would you feel if you were a disciple and heard Jesus saying, "One of you will betray me?"

2. When you hear the word "Communion" what comes to your mind?

3. Why has Communion remained so important to Christians through the centuries?

PARENT PAGE

• Distribute page to parents.

Team Effort—Junior High! Middle School (15-20 Minutes)

The Communion Experience

- Much like baptism, the best "hands-on" experience is to participate in the sacrament of Eucharist, or Communion. Invite your pastor to provide Communion and perhaps discuss the significance of Communion in your tradition.
- Option: Do this "Team Effort" after the "In the Word" section.

Team Effort—High School (15-20 Minutes)

The Upper Room Experience

- Much like baptism, the best "hands-on" experiential education is to participate in the sacrament of Eucharist or Communion. Invite your pastor to provide Communion and perhaps discuss the significance of Communion in your own tradition. Here's a unique way to have Communion:
- Create an atmosphere of the Upper Room experience. (If you have an upstairs room, use it.) Place an extra long table with 13 chairs arranged around it to give your students a Communion experience similar to what you would have imagined the Upper Room to have looked like from John 13. Then bring 12 students in at a time (if you have less this room. Then pass the bread and cup around the table as you read the words of Communion found in Mark 14:12-26. Allow time for individual prayer and worship. The use of candlelight in a darkened room and worship music can help set a very special mood.
- Option: Move this "Team Effort" until after the "In the Word" section.

In the Word (25-30 Minutes)

The Last Supper

- Give each student a copy of "The Last Supper" on pages 109-111 and a pen or pencil, or display a copy using an overhead projector.
- Discuss Part I of the Bible study with the whole group.
- Divide students into three groups. Each group will discuss one section of Part II of the Bible study.
- Have students return to the whole group and share what they learned.

I. The Event

"On the first day of the Feast of Unleavened Bread, the disciples came to Jesus and asked, 'Where do you want us to make preparations for you to eat the Passover?'

"He replied, 'Go into the city to a certain man and tell him, "The Teacher says: My appointed time is near. I am going to celebrate the Passover with my disciples at your house."' So the disciples did as Jesus had directed them and prepared the Passover.

"When evening came, Jesus was reclining at the table with the Twelve. And while they were eating, he said, 'I tell you the truth, one of you will betray me.'

"They were very sad and began to say to him one after the other, 'Surely not I, Lord?'

"Jesus replied, 'The one who has dipped his hand into the bowl with me will betray me. The Son of Man will go just as it is written about him. But woe to that man who betrays the Son of Man! It would be better for him if he had not been born.'

"Then Judas, the one who would betray him, said, 'Surely not I, Rabbi?'

"Jesus answered, 'Yes, it is you.'

"While they were eating, Jesus took bread, gave thanks and broke it, and gave it to his disciples, saying, 'Take it and eat; this is my body.' Then he took the cup, gave thanks and offered it to them, saying, 'Drink from it, all of you. This is my blood of the covenant, which is poured out for many for the forgiveness of sins. I tell you, I will not drink of this fruit of the vine from now on until that day when I drink it anew with you in my Father's kingdom'" (Matthew 26:17-29).

Why is this event commonly called the "Last Supper?"

Why do you suppose this meal that Jesus had with His disciples would be considered a major event in His life?

II. Looking at the Event

Group One

A. The Passover Meal

Jesus was coming into the holy city of Jerusalem in order to participate in the sacred Passover celebration. To gain a better understanding of what Christians call Communion, or the Eucharist, we must understand a little of the Passover meal eaten at the Last Supper of Jesus before His crucifixion.

Read Exodus 12 in order to grasp what the Passover celebration is all about. Summarize the Passover in your own words in the space below.

Group Two

B. Judas's Betrayal Foretold

What did Jesus say about the person who would betray Him? (See Matthew 26:20-25.)

What took place in Matthew 26:47-50 and Matthew 27:3-5?

Now prepare to share this section with the whole group.

Group Three

C. The Lord's Supper Instituted

How were Jesus Christ's words, recorded in Matthew 26:26-29, a prophecy of His death?

What is the significance of the bread? The wine?

Now prepare to share this section with the whole group.

WARM UP

UNIQUE FOOD QUESTIONNAIRE

What is the weirdest food you have ever eaten?

....

....

What is the most bizarre combination of foods you have ever eaten?

....

....

What is the most food you have eaten at one time?

....

....

If you were on a desert island and could only eat one meal for a year what would it be?

....

....

What's the worst tasting food you have ever eaten?

....

....

IN THE WORD

THE LAST SUPPER

I. The Event

"On the first day of the Feast of Unleavened Bread, the disciples came to Jesus and asked, 'Where do you want us to make preparations for you to eat the Passover?'

"He replied, 'Go into the city to a certain man and tell him, "The Teacher says: My appointed time is near, I am going to celebrate the Passover with my disciples at your house."' So the disciples did as Jesus had directed them and prepared the Passover.

"When evening came, Jesus was reclining at the table with the Twelve. And while they were eating, he said, 'I tell you the truth, one of you will betray me.'

"They were very sad and began to say to him one after the other, 'Surely not I, Lord?'

"Jesus replied, 'The one who has dipped his hand into the bowl with me will betray me. The Son of Man will go just as it is written about him. But woe to that man who betrays the Son of Man! It would be better for him if he had not been born.'

"Then Judas, the one who would betray him, said, 'Surely not I, Rabbi?'

"Jesus answered, 'Yes, it is you.'

"While they were eating, Jesus took bread, gave thanks and broke it, and gave it to his disciples, saying, ' Take it and eat; this is my body.' Then he took the cup, gave thanks and offered it to them, saying, 'Drink from it, all of you. This is my blood of the covenant, which is poured out for many for the forgiveness of sins. I tell you, I will not drink of this fruit of the vine from now on until that day when I drink it anew with you in my Father's kingdom'" (Matthew 26:17-29).

Why is this event commonly called the "Last Supper?"

....

....

Why do you suppose this meal that Jesus had with His disciples would be considered a major event in His life?

....

....

II. Looking at the Event
Group One

A. The Passover Meal

Jesus was coming into the holy city of Jerusalem in order to participate in the sacred Passover celebration. To gain a better understanding of what Christians call Communion, or the Eucharist, we must understand a little of the Passover meal eaten at the Last Supper of Jesus before His crucifixion.

Read Exodus 12 in order to grasp what the Passover celebration is all about. Summarize the Passover in your own words in the space below.

....

....

....

IN THE WORD

Now prepare to share this section with the whole group.

Group Two

B.   Judas's Betrayal Foretold

What did Jesus say about the person who would betray Him? (See Matthew 26:20-25.)

....

What took place in Matthew 26:47-50 and Matthew 27:3-5?

....

Now prepare to share this section with the whole group.

Group Three

C.   The Lord's Supper Instituted

How were Jesus Christ's words, recorded in Matthew 26:26-29, a prophecy of His death?

....

....

What is the significance of the bread? The wine?

....

....

Why is Communion (the Eucharist) as special today as it was almost 2,000 years ago?

....

Now prepare to share this section with the whole group.

SO WHAT?

Many of the events of Jesus' life were recorded in the New Testament, but the Last Supper is one re-created and remembered regularly by Christians all over the earth. Participating in Communion is an act of remembrance that Jesus Christ's body was broken for you. He died so that you might live. It also means remembering that His blood was shed for you so that your sins would be forgiven. You are righteous before God only because of the broken Body and Blood of Jesus Christ.

When you realize that many thousands of Christians all over the world share with you in Communion, how do you feel?

....

....

What makes Communion special for you? If it is not special to you, if it has simply been a ritual, write down your feelings about that.

....

....

THINGS TO THINK ABOUT

1. How would you feel if you were a disciple and heard Jesus saying, "One of you will betray me?"

....

....

....

2. When you hear the word "Communion" what comes to your mind?

....

....

....

3. Why has Communion remained so important to Christians through the centuries?

....

....

....

PARENT PAGE

Communion can be a profound time—an intimate encounter with God. When we participate in the Eucharist, Christ is present. Once again we are reminded of His sacrificial love for us.

The next time you approach the Communion table, here are some things to think about:

1. Communion is a time of reflection on all that God has done for you and on His awesome demonstration of love. Take a few moments to reflect. Share your thoughts with your family.

....

....

2. Communion is a time of confession. When we stand in the presence of Christ we must confess our sins and shortcomings. To confess our sins to God means to agree with Him that we miss the mark of His perfection and need Him to be our Savior and Forgiver. Take some time to confess your sins to God. You may write them in the space below if you wish, or share them with your family.

....

....

....

"Therefore confess your sins to each other and pray for each other so that you may be healed" (James 5:16). When you are finished confessing your sins, read 1 John 1:9. What is the good news of this verse?

....

....

3. Communion is a time of dedication. Whenever we are aware of the ultimate sacrifice of love, Christ shedding His blood and dying on a cross on our behalf, we are drawn to dedicate our lives to Him and to be reconciled to Him. Share with your family what you are dedicating to God. Take a few moments to pray. Tell God of your love for Him and your commitment to Him.

4. Communion is a time of praise. We can praise and thank God for His unconditional love. Communion reminds us of His kindness and goodness to our sinful world. Write in the space below your praise to God and then share with your family.

....

....

"Let everything that has breath praise the Lord" (Psalm 150:6).

Session 7 "The Last Supper"

Date ....

THE CRUCIFIXION OF JESUS CHRIST

K EY VERSES

"They came to a place called Golgotha (which means The Place of the Skull). There they offered Jesus wine to drink, mixed with gall; but after tasting it, he refused to drink it. When they had crucified him, they divided up his clothes by casting lots. And sitting down, they kept watch over him there. Above his head they placed the written charge against him: THIS IS JESUS, THE KING OF THE JEWS. Two robbers were crucified with him, one on his right and one on his left."
Matthew 27:33-38

B IBLICAL BASIS

Psalm 22;
Matthew 27:27-44;
Mark 15:16-32;
Luke 23:26-43;
John 19:16-27;
Romans 5:6-8;
1 Peter 2:21-25

T HE BIG IDEA

The Crucifixion is the condemnation of Jesus Christ as a criminal, but more importantly, the point in history where the sin of humanity is confronted by the love of God.

A IMS OF THIS SESSION

During this session you will guide students to:
• Examine the crucifixion and sacrificial death of Jesus of Nazareth;
• Discover how Jesus' death on the cross was the ultimate sacrifice of God for humankind;
• Implement a plan to rethink how the crucifixion of Jesus and the sacrificial love of God relate to their commitments to Christ.

W ARM UP

SACRIFICE—
A look at the meaning of sacrifice.

T EAM EFFORT— JUNIOR HIGH/ MIDDLE SCHOOL

THE CRUCIFIXION ON SCREEN!—
A discussion following the viewing of a scene of the Crucifixion.

T EAM EFFORT— HIGH SCHOOL

BUILD A CROSS—
Students build a cross.

I N THE WORD

THE CRUCIFIXION OF JESUS CHRIST—
A Bible study on the events and prophecy of the Crucifixion of Jesus Christ.

T HINGS TO THINK ABOUT (OPTIONAL)

Questions to get students thinking and talking about their responses to Christ's suffering for their sakes.

P ARENT PAGE

A tool to get the session into the home and allow parents and young people to discuss the effects of the events of Christ's Crucifixion on each individual.

LEADER'S DEVOTIONAL

"You see, at just the right time, when we were still powerless, Christ died for the ungodly. Very rarely will anyone die for a righ–teous man, though for a good man someone might possibly dare to die. But God demonstrates his own love for us in this: While we were still sinners, Christ died for us" (Romans 5:6-8).

As the son of a mortician, I grew up with death all around me. Yes, my dad is really a funeral director. Physically speaking, he is the guy who makes sure you have an eternal resting place, whether that place is a hole in the ground or your ashes scattered on the Pacific Ocean.

I never really developed an appreciation for death, not that I was eager to experience it, until I became a Christian when I was 16 years old. Death never really had a strong impact on my life until I understood the significance of Christ's sacrificial death on the cross for me. Without God, I realized that not only was I unprepared for eternal life, but I was headed for sure and certain eternal death.

My dad has buried lots of people who have died in all kinds of horrible and tragic ways. But he's never buried anyone who's died through the torture and agony of crucifix- ion. Despite all the deaths I've heard about, nothing can compare to the injustice of the beating, whipping, mocking, spitting and crucifying of my Lord. What makes Christ's painful death even more unbelievable is the truth that He was completely innocent.

The sacrifice of Jesus displayed in His crucifixion is God's signature for His love for you. Death has been defeated by the power of God and every blow Jesus took was a blow against the sin of this world. The Cross is not a symbol of death, but a sign of victory. Even a gruesome instrument of death designed to kill a King could not conquer the king- dom of God. As you and your students reflect on the crucifixion of Christ in this lesson, remember that Christ's death was to free you from your death. In Christ, you are headed for sure and certain eternal life. (Written by Joey O'Connor.)

"Even after generations of people had spit in his face, he still loved them. After a nation of chosen ones had stripped him naked and ripped his incarnated flesh, he still died for them. And even today, after billions have cho- sen to prostitute them- selves before pimps of power, fame, and wealth, he still waits for them."
—Max Lucado

THE CRUCIFIXION OF JESUS CHRIST

KEY VERSES

"They came to a place called Golgotha (which means The Place of the Skull). There they offered Jesus wine to drink, mixed with gall; but after tasting it, he refused to drink it. When they had crucified him, they divided up his clothes by casting lots. And sitting down, they kept watch over him there. Above his head they placed the written charge against him: THIS IS JESUS, THE KING OF THE JEWS. Two robbers were crucified with him, one on his right and one on his left." Matthew 27:33-38

BIBLICAL BASIS

Psalm 22; Matthew 27:27-44; Mark 15:16-32; Luke 23:26-43; John 19:16-27; Romans 5:6-8; 1 Peter 2:21-25

THE BIG IDEA

The Crucifixion is the condemnation of Jesus Christ as a criminal, but more importantly, the point in history where the sin of humanity is confronted by the love of God.

WARM UP (5-10 MINUTES)
SACRIFICE

• Divide students into groups of three or four.
• Give each student a copy of "Sacrifice" on page 121 and a pen or pencil.
• Have students discuss the questions and statements in their groups.

When you think of the word "sacrifice," what comes to your mind?

Name someone who has sacrificed something for you.

Describe a time when you sacrificed something for someone else.

How does looking at these similarities affect your faith in God?

SO WHAT?
Christ's Sacrificial Love

How was the death of Christ a sacrifice of love for you?

Because of His death, what are your benefits?

What is your response?

THINGS TO THINK ABOUT (OPTIONAL)

• Use the questions on page 127 after or as a part of "In the Word."

1. How would you feel if you were a disciple of Jesus and you had watched Him die on the cross?

2. How does the knowledge of Christ's suffering on the cross help you understand the depth of love God has for you?

3. Beyond His physical suffering, what did Jesus bear in His death?

PARENT PAGE

• Distribute page to parents.

What images come to your mind when you think of the sacrificial love of God?

TEAM EFFORT—JUNIOR HIGH

MIDDLE SCHOOL (15-20 Minutes)

THE CRUCIFIXION ON SCREEN!

- Rent a video of *The Jesus Film*, *Jesus*, *The Robe*, *Jesus of Nazareth*, Michael W. Smith's video *Secret Ambition* or any similar video available at a local video store. Show the portion of the film with the Crucifixion scene. Then discuss: their impressions, their feelings, the love of Christ, His pain and His sacrifice.

TEAM EFFORT—HIGH SCHOOL (15-20 Minutes)

BUILD A CROSS

This exercise will help your group identify with the pain of the Cross and the sacrificial love of God. Pass out a nail to each person. Spikes are even better. Then provide two large pieces of wood and some hammers. Have the students build a cross (or if it is a large group, build several crosses) to keep as a reminder of God's sacrificial love. When the group has built a cross, have each student write a message to Christ on a part of the wood. The messages can be as simple as "thank you," a verse or anything that is meaningful to them.

IN THE WORD (25-30 Minutes)

THE CRUCIFIXION OF JESUS CHRIST

- Divide students into groups of three or four.
- Give each student a copy of "The Crucifixion of Jesus Christ" on pages 123-125 and a pen or pencil, or display a copy using an overhead projector.
- Have students complete the Bible study.

I. The Event

"Then the governor's soldiers took Jesus into the Praetorium and gathered the whole company of soldiers around him. They stripped him and put a scarlet robe on him, and then twisted together a crown of thorns and set it on his head. They put a staff in his right hand and knelt in front of him and mocked him. 'Hail, King of the Jews!' they said. They spit on him, and took the staff and struck him on the head again and again. After they had mocked him, they took off the robe and put his own clothes on him. Then they led him away to crucify him.

As they were going out, they met a man from Cyrene, named Simon, and they forced him to carry the cross. They came to a place called Golgotha (which means The Place of the Skull). There they offered Jesus wine to drink, mixed with gall; but after tasting it, he refused to drink it. When they had crucified him, they divided up his clothes by casting lots. And sitting down, they kept watch over him there. Above his head they placed the written charge against him: THIS IS JESUS, THE KING OF THE JEWS. Two robbers were crucified with him, one on his right and one on his left. Those who passed by hurled insults at him, shaking their heads and saying, 'You who are going to destroy the temple and build it in three days, save yourself! Come down from the cross, if you are the Son of God!'

"In the same way the chief priests, the teachers of the law and the elders mocked him. 'He saved others,' they said, 'but he can't save himself! He's the king of Israel! Let him come down now from the cross, and we will believe in him. He trusts in God. Let God rescue him now if he wants him, for he said, "I am the Son of God."' In the same way the robbers who were crucified with him also heaped insults on him" (Matthew 27:27-44).

Crucifixion (hanging on a cross) was the Roman method of execution for slaves and foreigners. Generally it took a very long time for a person to die on a cross, therefore making it excruciatingly painful. Death by crucifixion was unspeakably shameful and degrading. Yet Jesus Christ willingly suffered through the physical pain and humiliation of the cross in order for humankind to be set free from sin. After reading about the crucifixion of Jesus Christ, what are your feelings and impressions about Jesus?

Matthew 27:27-31 describes how Jesus was physically beaten and mocked before He was crucified. What do you imagine He was feeling—physically, emotionally and psychologically—during this ordeal of abuse?

II. Looking at the Event
From reading the different accounts of the Crucifixion, what new insights do you gain from the other Gospels?
Mark 15:16-32

Luke 23:26-43

John 19:16-27

A. The Thief and Jesus
Read Luke 23:39-43. What do you think Jesus meant when He said "Today you will be with me in paradise" (v. 43)?

What implications does this conversation have for our lives?

B. The Event Foretold
Compare Matthew 27:35 and Psalm 22:16-18.
Psalm 22 was written hundreds of years before the crucifixion of Jesus, yet it contains amazingly detailed prophecy of what happened at the Cross. Read Psalm 22 and jot down any similarities you see to the crucifixion of Jesus.

WARM UP

SACRIFICE

When you think of the word "sacrifice," what comes to your mind?

....
....
....

Name someone who has sacrificed something for you.

....
....
....

Describe a time when you sacrificed something for someone else.

....
....
....

What images come to your mind when you think of the sacrificial love of God?

....
....
....

THE CRUCIFIXION OF JESUS CHRIST

I. **The Event**

"Then the governor's soldiers took Jesus into the Praetorium and gathered the whole company of soldiers around him. They stripped him and put a scarlet robe on him, and then twisted together a crown of thorns and set it on his head. They put a staff in his right hand and knelt in front of him and mocked him. 'Hail, King of the Jews!' they said. They spit on him, and took the staff and struck him on the head again and again. After they had mocked him, they took off the robe and put his own clothes on him. Then they led him away to crucify him.

"As they were going out, they met a man from Cyrene, named Simon, and they forced him to carry the cross. They came to a place called Golgotha (which means The Place of the Skull). There they offered Jesus wine to drink, mixed with gall; but after tasting it, he refused to drink it. When they had crucified him, they divided up his clothes by casting lots. And sitting down, they kept watch over him there. Above his head they placed the written charge against him: THIS IS JESUS, THE KING OF THE JEWS. Two robbers were crucified with him, one on his right and one on his left. Those who passed by hurled insults at him, shaking their heads and saying, 'You who are going to destroy the temple and build it in three days, save yourself! Come down from the cross, if you are the Son of God!'

"In the same way the chief priests, the teachers of the law and the elders mocked him. 'He saved others,' they said, 'but he can't save himself! He's the king of Israel! Let him come down now from the cross, and we will believe in him. He trusts in God. Let God rescue him now if he wants him, for he said, "I am the Son of God."' In the same way the robbers who were crucified with him also heaped insults on him" (Matthew 27:27-44).

Crucifixion (hanging on a cross) was the Roman method of execution for slaves and foreigners. Generally it took a very long time for a person to die on a cross, therefore making it excruciatingly painful. Death by crucifixion was unspeakably shameful and degrading. Yet Jesus Christ willingly suffered through the physical pain and humiliation of the cross in order for humankind to be set free from sin.

After reading about the crucifixion of Jesus Christ, what are your feelings and impressions about Jesus?

....

....

Matthew 27:27-31 describes how Jesus was physically beaten and mocked before He was crucified. What do you imagine He was feeling—physically, emotionally and psychologically—during this ordeal of abuse?

....

....

 N THE WORD

THE CRUCIFIXION OF
JESUS CHRIST

II.   Looking at the Event
From reading the different accounts of the Crucifixion, what new insights do you gain
from the other Gospels?

Mark 15:16-32 ....

....

Luke 23:26-43 ....

....

John 19:16-27 ....

....

A.   The Thief and Jesus
Read Luke 23:39-43. What do you think Jesus meant when He said "Today you will be with me in paradise"
(v. 43)?

....

....

What implications does this conversation have for our lives?

....

....

B.   The Event Foretold
Compare Matthew 27:35 and Psalm 22:16-18.

....

....

Psalm 22 was written hundreds of years before the crucifixion of Jesus, yet it contains
amazingly detailed prophecy of what happened at the Cross.

Read Psalm 22 and jot down any similarities you see to the crucifixion of Jesus.

....

....

....

How does looking at these similarities affect your faith in God?

....

....

....

So What?

Christ's Sacrificial Love

How was the death of Christ a sacrifice of love for you?

....

....

....

Because of His death, what are your benefits?

....

....

....

What is your response?

....

....

....

....

Things to Think About

1. How would you feel if you were a disciple of Jesus and you had watched Him die on the cross?

....

....

2. How does the knowledge of Christ's suffering on the cross help you understand the depth of love God has for you?

....

....

....

3. Beyond His physical suffering, what did Jesus bear in His death?

....

....

....

....

PARENT PAGE

THE CRUCIFIXION

If you were one of the disciples of Jesus and you watched Him first being mocked and physically beaten, then struggling to carry the cross to Golgotha, and finally, hanging on that cross suffering, what thoughts would be going on in your mind?

....

....

....

How does the knowledge of Christ's suffering on the cross help you to understand the depth of His love for you?

....

....

....

Read 1 Peter 2:21-25. How does this Scripture help you better understand Christ's suffering for you?

....

....

....

What do you think verse 21 means?

....

....

....

Reread verse 24. How does this verse summarize the crucifixion of Jesus?

....

....

....

Session 8 "The Crucifixion of Jesus Christ"
Date ....

SACRIFICIAL LOVE

LEADER'S PEP TALK

When I was a youth pastor at a large church in California, I got the shock of my ministry. One year right before Easter, I gave the students in our Sunday School class a pop quiz. The surprise came when most of the students flunked the test on the life and ministry of Jesus Christ. Every week we sang about Him, we prayed to Him and teens confessed their faith in Christ as their Messiah. But in droves they couldn't communicate clearly the reasons for the birth, death and resurrection of their Lord. Few could even take a guess at what the Incarnation meant and, even though most had been baptized, many weren't sure of the biblical reasons for baptism. To be honest, I felt like a failure as a youth worker. If my students couldn't even talk intelligently about Jesus, was it worth it?

That Easter as we studied once again the wonderful fact that "Christ is risen, He has risen indeed!" I watched some of our students "get it." This section of the study isn't about the bloody, painful death of Jesus or even just about the facts surrounding the empty tomb. It's not about the incredible promise at the Ascension or the wonderful promise of His second coming. This section is about sacrificial love and redemption. It's about a price that was paid on a cross so that we might live abundantly and eternally. In the midst of the lessons, don't let the students miss the greatest love story that will ever be written. Jesus of Nazareth is our Savior, our Hope.

One of my favorite authors, Max Lucado, received a Christmas card with words that pretty much sum it up.

> If our greatest need had been information, God
> would have sent an educator.
> If our greatest need had been technology, God would
> have sent us a scientist.
> If our greatest need had been money, God would
> have sent us an economist. But since our greatest
> need was forgiveness, God sent us a Savior.

What a privilege we have to introduce and reintroduce these amazing love stories to our students. If you are anything like me, you may get discouraged at times because some of the students after all these years still do not completely understand the simple stories from the life of our Savior, but don't give up yet. There is someone in your group who has been waiting all his or her life for you to teach these wonderful stories because this is the year he or she will get it. And for all eternity that person will thank you for being there for him or her.

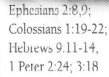

THE DEATH OF CHRIST

KEY VERSES

"At the sixth hour darkness came over the whole land until the ninth hour. And at the ninth hour Jesus cried out in a loud voice, 'Eloi, Eloi, lama sabachthani?'—which means, 'My God, my God, why have you forsaken me?'

"When some of those standing near heard this, they said, 'Listen, he's calling Elijah.'

"One man ran, filled a sponge with wine vinegar, put it on a stick, and offered it to Jesus to drink. 'Now leave him alone. Let's see if Elijah comes to take him down,' he said.

"With a loud cry, Jesus breathed his last.

"The curtain of the temple was torn in two from top to bottom. And when the centurion, who stood there in front of Jesus, heard his cry and saw how he died, he said, 'Surely this man was the Son of God!'" Mark 15:33-39

BIBLICAL BASIS

Leviticus 16:29-34;
Psalm 22:1;
Mark 15:33-47;
John 3:16; 15:13; 19:30;
Romans 5:6-8; 3:21-25;
2 Corinthians 5:21;
Ephesians 2:8,9;
Colossians 1:19-22;
Hebrews 9:11-14,
1 Peter 2:24; 3:18

THE BIG IDEA

The death of Christ is the darkest moment in history turned into the greatest demonstration of love and hope the world has ever known.

AIMS OF THIS SESSION

During this session you will guide students to:
• Examine the biblical account of the death of Jesus;
• Discover how the death of Christ demonstrates God's unconditional love and offers the hope of eternal life through Christ;
• Implement a decision to understand the depth of God's love and apply that love to a deeper faith in Christ.

WARM UP

THE EULOGY OF JESUS OF NAZARETH—
Students write a eulogy for Jesus.

TEAM EFFORT— JUNIOR HIGH/ MIDDLE SCHOOL

GIVING TO OTHERS—
A story that demonstrates sacrificial love.

TEAM EFFORT— HIGH SCHOOL

NO GUTS, NO GLORY—
A description of the horrors of crucifixion.

IN THE WORD

THE DEATH OF CHRIST—
A Bible study on the meaning of Christ's death.

THINGS TO THINK ABOUT (OPTIONAL)

Questions to get students thinking and talking about God's sacrificial love demonstrated in Christ's crucifixion.

PARENT PAGE

A tool to get the session into the home and allow parents and young people to discuss the impact of the Crucifixion on their lives.

LEADER'S DEVOTIONAL

"When he had received the drink, Jesus said, 'It is finished.' With that, he bowed his head and gave up his spirit" (John 19:30).

For that one impossible student who ignores your every attempt to love him, Jesus cried, "It is finished." For the girl in your youth ministry with bulimia and a terrible self-image, Jesus cried, "It is finished." For the lonely, overweight boy with no social skills, Jesus cried, "It is finished." For the sweet, friendly girl who lives in an oppressive, legalistic, religious home, Jesus cried, "It is finished." For the ordinary teenager who struggles with gossip, impure thoughts and peer pressure, Jesus cried, "It is finished." For you, a sometimes tired and frustrated youth worker who wonders if your life is really making a difference, Jesus cried, "It is finished."

It is finished.

That's all we really need to know. When Jesus said "It is finished," it *was* finished. His death on the cross was the beginning of the end of every sin, frustration, tear, sadness, pain or trouble we experience. For every moment you feel like you're making no progress with the students you work with, Jesus' death can also put to death every thought of fear or worry you have. His death is the turning point of all history…of your history. His death is the ultimate sign of love and sacrifice for this world's rebellion against God. Anything not hidden in the shadow of the Cross stands exposed in the light of God. Because of the Cross, you can bring every student before God and trust Him to finish His work in their lives. You can also be assured that He is going to complete His work in you as well. Because of Jesus' sacrificial love, you can rejoice and agree with Him…*it is finished.* (Written by Joey O'Connor.)

"People say they are tired of life; no man was ever tired of life; the truth is that we are tired of being half dead while we are alive. What we need is to be transfigured by the incoming of a great and new life."
—Oswald Chambers

THE DEATH OF CHRIST

KEY VERSES

"At the sixth hour darkness came over the whole land until the ninth hour. And at the ninth hour Jesus cried out in a loud voice, *'Eloi, Eloi, lama sabachthani?'*—which means, 'My God, my God, why have you forsaken me?'

"When some of those standing near heard this, they said, 'Listen, he's calling Elijah.'

"One man ran, filled a sponge with wine vinegar, put it on a stick, and offered it to Jesus to drink. 'Now leave him alone. Let's see if Elijah comes to take him down,' he said.

"With a loud cry, Jesus breathed his last.

"The curtain of the temple was torn in two from top to bottom. And when the centurion, who stood there in front of Jesus, heard his cry and saw how he died, he said, 'Surely this man was the Son of God!'" Mark 15:33-39

BIBLICAL BASIS

Leviticus 16:29-34; Psalm 22:1; Mark 15:33-47; John 3:16; 15:13; 19:30; Romans 5:6-8; 3:21-25; 2 Corinthians 5:21; Ephesians 2:8,9; Colossians 1:19-22; Hebrews 9:11-14; 1 Peter 2:24, 3:18

THE BIG IDEA

The death of Christ is the darkest moment in history turned into the greatest demonstration of love and hope the world has ever known.

WARM UP (5-10 MINUTES)

THE EULOGY OF JESUS OF NAZARETH

• Divide students into groups of three or four.

• Give each group a copy of "The Eulogy of Jesus of Nazareth" on page 137 and a pen or pencil.

• Have students complete the activity.

• Have groups read their eulogies aloud. Imagine yourself at the funeral for Jesus of Nazareth. You don't know yet about the resurrection of Jesus. Your job as a group is to come up with a eulogy that would best describe the life of Christ and His death on a cross. As a group, come up with the contents of this eulogy.

Fold

---

sinned." You as a believer are justified and righteous before God, not because of your good works, but because of Christ's sacrifice on the cross.
Read Romans 5:1. What is the result of being justified in Christ?

Atonement—"to cover or pardon."
Atonement is another way of saying your sins are forgiven. Christ paid the price of death in order for you to be spiritually alive. Your atonement as a believer means that your guilt and sin have been removed. Christ's death on the cross (the shedding of blood) took the place of your spiritual death, and set you free. In the Old Testament, the Day of Atonement was one of the major religious days of the year. Read Leviticus 16:29-34. What happened on this day, according to verse 30?

How often were the people's sins atoned for, or forgiven, according to verse 34?

How has the death of Christ in the New Testament become our atonement? Read 2 Corinthians 5:21 and 1 Peter 2:24.

The New Testament form of atonement is reconciliation. Reconciliation means to change a person from enmity to friendship. According to Colossians 1:19-22, how has the process of reconciliation taken place for you?

So What?
The Death of Christ and You
According to 1 Peter 3:18, why did Christ die?

How does Ephesians 2:8,9 fit in to this understanding of the death of Christ?

What can you do in order for the death of Christ to become relevant to your life?

THINGS TO THINK ABOUT (OPTIONAL)

• Use the questions on page 147 after or as a part of "In the Word."

1. How does it make you feel knowing that Christ's physical death has reconciled you with God?

2. Which is a more meaningful symbol for you, the picture of Christ suffering on the cross before death or the picture of an empty cross with Christ resurrected? Why?

3. Describe in your own words the sacrificial love of God we see through the death of Christ.

PARENT PAGE

• Distribute page to parents.

Dearly beloved, we are gathered together today in the presence of God and the family and friends of our Master, Jesus of Nazareth...

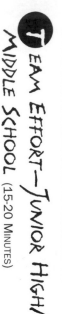

TEAM EFFORT—JUNIOR HIGH/MIDDLE SCHOOL (15-20 Minutes)

GIVING TO OTHERS

• Read the following story to the entire group, then discuss the questions.

A little boy was told by his doctor that he could actually save his sister's life by giving her some blood. The six-year-old girl was near death, a victim of disease from which the boy had made a marvelous recovery two years earlier. Her only chance for restoration was a blood transfusion from someone who had previously conquered the illness. Since the two children had the same rare blood type, the boy was the ideal donor.

"Johnny, would you like to give your blood for Mary?" the doctor asked. The boy hesitated. His lower lip started to tremble. Then he smiled and said, "Sure, Doc, I'll give my blood for my sister."

Soon the two children were wheeled into the operating room—Mary, pale and thin; Johnny, robust and the picture of health. Neither spoke, but when their eyes met, Johnny grinned.

As his blood siphoned into Mary's veins, one could almost see new life come into her tired body. The ordeal was almost over when Johnny's brave little voice broke the silence, "Say, Doc, when do I die?"

It was only then that the doctor realized what the moment of hesitation, the trembling of the lip, had meant earlier. Little Johnny actually thought that in giving his blood to his sister he was giving up his life! And in that brief moment, he had made his great decision!

How does this story display sacrificial love?

Why is blood so important in this story and in the death of Christ? (See Hebrews 9:11-14.)

Can you think of any other stories where displays of love and sacrifice had blood in them?

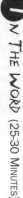

TEAM EFFORT—HIGH SCHOOL (15-20 Minutes)

No Guts, No Glory

• Give each student a copy of "No Guts, No Glory" on pages 139-141 and allow them time to read the article.
• Option: Have student volunteers take turns reading the article aloud.
• Have students share their answers to the question.

IN THE WORD (25-30 Minutes)

THE DEATH OF CHRIST

• Divide students into groups of three or four.
• Give each student a copy of "The Death of Christ" on pages 143-147 and a pen or pencil, or display a copy using an overhead projector.
• Have students complete the Bible study.

I. The Event

"At the sixth hour darkness came over the whole land until the ninth hour. And at the ninth hour Jesus cried out in a loud voice, 'Eloi, Eloi, lama sabachthani?'—which means, 'My God, my God, why have you forsaken me?'

"When some of those standing near heard this, they said, 'Listen, he's calling Elijah.'

"One man ran, filled a sponge with wine vinegar, put it on a stick, and offered it to Jesus to drink. 'Now leave him alone. Let's see if Elijah comes to take him down,' he said.

"With a loud cry, Jesus breathed his last.

"The curtain of the temple was torn in two from top to bottom. And when the centurion, who stood there in front of Jesus, heard his cry and saw how he died, he said, 'Surely this man was the Son of God!'

"Some women were watching from a distance. Among them were Mary Magdalene, Mary the mother of James the younger and of Joses, and Salome. In Galilee these women had followed him and cared for his needs. Many other women who had come up with him to Jerusalem were also there.

"It was Preparation Day (that is, the day before the Sabbath). So as evening approached, Joseph of Arimathea, a prominent member of the Council, who was himself waiting for the kingdom of God, went boldly to Pilate and asked for Jesus' body. Pilate was surprised to hear that he was already dead. Summoning the centurion, he asked him if Jesus had already died. When he learned from the centurion that it was so, he gave the body to Joseph. So Joseph bought some linen cloth, took down the body, wrapped it in the linen, and placed it in a tomb cut out of rock. Then he rolled a stone against the entrance of the tomb. Mary Magdalene and Mary the mother of Joses saw where he was laid" (Mark 15:33-47).

It is incredible how God took the darkest moment in world history and turned it into the greatest demonstration of love and hope the world has ever known.

According to Mark 15:34 (see also Psalm 22:1), "Jesus cried out with a loud voice, 'My God, my God, why have you forsaken me.'" Why do you think He said that, and what did He mean by these words?

Why do you suppose the Roman centurion made the statement recorded in Mark 15:39?

Using your imagination, write out a few thoughts on what the people in verse 40 might have been doing or talking about at this time and share them with your group.

II. Looking at the Event

A. Why Christ Died

Let us look at the following verses to discover and explore the purpose of Christ's death on the cross. After each section of Scripture, write down your understanding of why Christ died.

John 3:16

Romans 3:21-25

Romans 5:6-8

B. The Result of the Death of Christ

Because Jesus Christ sacrificed His life on the cross almost 2,000 years ago, you have the opportunity to be set free from your sins and be called a child of God. Jesus Christ had to bear the sins of the world while on the cross to bridge the gap between the holiness of God and the sinfulness of humankind.

Here are a few "theological" words that will help you comprehend the meaning of the death of Jesus Christ.

Justification—"to be made right."

Justification refers to the believer's relationship with God. Because of Christ's death, the believer in Christ can be made right with God. An easy way to remember what it means is to think of it as "just-as-if-I'd-never-

THE DEATH OF CHRIST

THE EULOGY OF JESUS OF NAZARETH

Imagine yourself at the funeral for Jesus of Nazareth. You don't know yet about the resurrection of Jesus. Your job as a group is to come up with a eulogy that would best describe the life of Christ and His death on a cross.

As a group, come up with the contents of this eulogy.

Dearly beloved, we are gathered together today in the presence of God and the family and friends of our Master, Jesus of Nazareth...

....

....

....

....

....

THE DEATH OF CHRIST

TEAM EFFORT

NO GUTS, NO GLORY [1]

A medical doctor writes about the physical pain of Jesus on the cross.
By Edward R. Bloomquist, M.D.

Like many others of His era, Jesus died on a cross by decree of Roman officials and endured one of man's most fierce tortures. But unlike others, He also bore the sins of the world on His sinless body—a spiritual agony we cannot begin to comprehend. We can, however, sense to a small degree His physical suffering.

Once in the tribunal area, the victim was stripped and his hands tied above his head to a supporting column. A soldier was stationed on each side of the condemned, and they took turns beating him with a flagrum—a short handle equipped with leather thongs whose ends were tipped with lead balls or sheep bones.

The thongs fell where they would, the leather strips burying themselves deep in the victim's body. When wrenched away, the lead balls ripped out bits of flesh. Hemorrhaging was intense, and the destruction of the condemned's body so extensive that even some Roman soldiers, hardened to brutality, were revolted.

National law prohibited more than 40 lashes. Ever cautious to uphold the law, Pharisees demanded the beatings be stopped at the 39th stroke. Rome had only one stipulation: The prisoner must remain alive and capable of carrying his crossbar to the execution.

Once the beating was completed, the near-naked victim was jerked to his feet, and the crossbar (weighing some 125 pounds) was laid on his shoulders. The condemned's arms were lashed to the crossbar, preventing a dash for freedom or striking out at his adversaries. A rope was commonly tied around his waist to direct his progress as he struggled through the streets. Romans preferred their victims naked; it was more humiliating. National preference, however, called for some clothing. The Romans usually agreed to this request by providing a loincloth.

Once the execution spot was reached, onlookers were held back and the victim was forced to the base of the stake. Then the crossbeam was removed from his back and experienced attendants threw him on the ground, grabbing his hands and stretching them out on the crossbar for size. The executioner placed an auger under each outstretched hand, and drilled a hole for the large crucifixion nail— a square spike about a third of an inch thick at its head.

The nail point was placed at the heel of the victim's hand. A single blow sent it ripping through the tissue, separating the carpal bones as it plunged into the crossbar. Paintings usually show the nail through the palm. Anatomically, this is impractical; the tissue cannot bear weight, and the victims would drop to the ground within minutes after being elevated.

Usually, the nail tore through the median nerve, creating an unending trail of fire up the victim's arms, augmenting the pain that tortured his body. From this moment on, this pain would intensify each time the victim moved, for the metal irritated the open nerve endings.

TEAM EFFORT

Once the victim was in place, the plaque that had proceeded him was nailed to the crossbar, which was then elevated and, with a thud, dropped into place on the pointed stake.

Before the elevation, the condemned man's arms formed a 90-degree angle with his body. After elevation, the sag caused by the weight of an average man's body decreased this angle to 65 degrees, exerting a tremendous pull on each nail.

There was no need to nail the feet, but the guards were usually irritated by the inevitable flailing. To prevent this, they put one foot over the other and drove a nail through both. But this merely prolonged death.

If the Romans didn't nail the feet, the victim's body would hang on its arms, causing it to go into a spasm that prevented exhalation. The victim soon suffocated from an inability to use his respiratory muscles. The foot nail changed this. The urge to survive is ever present, even on the cross. It didn't take long for the crucified to discover he could exhale if he lifted himself on the nail in his feet. This was intensely painful, but the desire to breathe overcame the horror of the pain. This alternating lift and drop maneuver became a reflex action after a few hours. It could prolong life for as much as two days, depending on the individual's strength and determination. To this extent, the perpetuation of his life rested in the willpower of the crucified.

As the hours wore on, the victim's mental faculties were impaired. His body became soaked with sweat. Thirst became intense. Pain and shock were tremendous. This pathetic picture continued until the victim died.

Such was the horror of the crucifixion as Jesus dragged Himself from His knees in the Garden of Gethsemane to Golgotha. He had told His disciples—and this they could understand—that a man has no greater love than to lay down his life for his friends. (See John 15:13.) Before long they'd understand a love that surpasses even this—a love so divine that He laid down His life for His enemies as well.

What emotions, feelings and thoughts come to your mind as you read this account of the Crucifixion?

....

....

....

Note:

Adapted from Edward R. Bloomquist, M.D., "No Guts, No Glory," *Breakaway,* (April 1992): 21-22.

THE DEATH OF
CHRIST

IN THE WORD

THE DEATH OF CHRIST

I. The Event

"At the sixth hour darkness came over the whole land until the ninth hour. And at the ninth hour Jesus cried out in a loud voice, *'Eloi, Eloi, lama sabachthani?'*—which means, 'My God, my God, why have you forsaken me?'

"When some of those standing near heard this, they said, 'Listen, he's calling Elijah.'

"One man ran, filled a sponge with wine vinegar, put it on a stick, and offered it to Jesus to drink. 'Now leave him alone. Let's see if Elijah comes to take him down,' he said.

"With a loud cry, Jesus breathed his last.

"The curtain of the temple was torn in two from top to bottom. And when the centurion, who stood there in front of Jesus, heard his cry and saw how he died, he said, 'Surely this man was the Son of God!'

"Some women were watching from a distance. Among them were Mary Magdalene, Mary the mother of James the younger and of Joses, and Salome. In Galilee these women had followed him and cared for his needs. Many other women who had come up with him to Jerusalem were also there."

"It was Preparation Day (that is, the day before the Sabbath). So as evening approached, Joseph of Arimathea, a prominent member of the Council, who was himself waiting for the kingdom of God, went boldly to Pilate and asked for Jesus' body. Pilate was surprised to hear that he was already dead. Summoning the centurion, he asked him if Jesus had already died. When he learned from the centurion that it was so, he gave the body to Joseph. So Joseph bought some linen cloth, took down the body, wrapped it in the linen, and placed it in a tomb cut out of rock. Then he rolled a stone against the entrance of the tomb. Mary Magdalene and Mary the mother of Joses saw where he was laid" (Mark 15:33-47).

It is incredible how God took the darkest moment in world history and turned it into the greatest demonstration of love and hope the world has ever known.

According to Mark 15:34 (see also Psalm 22:1), "Jesus cried out in a loud voice, 'My God, my God, why have you forsaken me?'" Why do you think He said that, and what did He mean by these words?

....

....

....

Why do you suppose the Roman centurion made the statement recorded in Mark 15:39?

....

....

....

IN THE WORD

Using your imagination, write out a few thoughts on what the people in verse 40 might have been doing or talking about at this time and share them with your group.

....

....

II. Looking at the Event

A. Why Christ Died

Let us look at the following verses to discover and explore the purpose of Christ's death on the cross. After each section of Scripture, write down your understanding of why Christ died.

John 3:16 ....

....

....

Romans 3:21-25 ....

....

....

Romans 5:6-8 ....

....

....

B. The Result of the Death of Christ

Because Jesus Christ sacrificed His life on the cross almost 2,000 years ago, you have the opportunity to be set free from your sins and be called a child of God. Jesus Christ had to bear the sins of the world while on the cross to bridge the gap between the holiness of God and the sinfulness of humankind.

Here are a few "theological" words that will help you comprehend the meaning of the death of Jesus Christ:

Justification—"to be made right."

Justification refers to the believer's relationship with God. Because of Christ's death, the believer in Christ can be made right with God. An easy way to remember what it means is to think of it as "just-as-if-I'd-never-sinned." You as a believer are justified and righteous before God, not because of your good works, but because of Christ's sacrifice on the cross.

Read Romans 5:1. What is the result of being justified in Christ?

....

....

Atonement—"to cover or pardon."

Atonement is another way of saying your sins are forgiven. Christ paid the price of death in order for you to be spiritually alive. Your atonement as a believer means that

THE DEATH OF CHRIST

 IN THE WORD

your guilt and sin have been removed. Christ's death on the cross (the shedding of blood) took the place of your spiritual death, and set you free.

In the Old Testament, the Day of Atonement was one of the major religious days of the year. Read Leviticus 16:29-34. What happened on this day, according to verse 30?

....

....

How often were the people's sins atoned for, or forgiven, according to verse 34?

....

How has the death of Christ in the New Testament become our atonement? Read 2 Corinthians 5:21 and 1 Peter 2:24.

....

....

The New Testament form of atonement is reconciliation. Reconciliation means to change a person from enmity to friendship. According to Colossians 1:19-22, how has the process of reconciliation taken place for you?

....

....

SO WHAT?
The Death of Christ and You
According to 1 Peter 3:18, why did Christ die?

....

....

....

How does Ephesians 2:8,9 fit in to this understanding of the death of Christ?

....

....

....

What can you do in order for the death of Christ to become relevant to your life?

....

....

....

THINGS TO THINK ABOUT

1. How does it make you feel knowing that Christ's physical death has reconciled you with God?

....

....

2. Which is a more meaningful symbol for you, the picture of Christ suffering on the cross before death or the picture of an empty cross with Christ resurrected? Why?

....

....

3. Describe in your own words the sacrificial love of God we see through the death of Christ.

....

....

THE DEATH OF CHRIST

THE DEATH OF CHRIST

Over nineteen hundred years ago in an obscure land, one Man died a common criminal's death on a cross. Yet that one Man's death has affected more lives than all of the other deaths before and after His.

How has His death impacted the world?

....

....

How has His death made an impact on your life?

....

....

"But God demonstrates his own love for us in this: While we were still sinners, Christ died for us." (Romans 5:8).

"For God so loved the world that he gave his one and only Son, that whoever believes in him shall not perish but have eternal life" (John 3:16).

How do these verses describe the sacrifice Christ made for us on the cross? What is the result of His sacrifice?

....

....

....

Session 9 "The Death of Christ"
Date ....

THE RESURRECTION

KEY VERSES

"After the Sabbath, at dawn on the first day of the week, Mary Magdalene and the other Mary went to look at the tomb.

"There was a violent earthquake, for an angel of the Lord came down from heaven and, going to the tomb, rolled back the stone and sat on it. His appearance was like lightning, and his clothes were white as snow. The guards were so afraid of him that they shook and became like dead men.

"The angel said to the women, 'Do not be afraid, for I know that you are looking for Jesus, who was crucified. He is not here; he has risen, just as he said. Come and see the place where he lay.'"
Matthew 28:1-6

BIBLICAL BASIS

Job 19:25-27;
Matthew 16:21; 17:22,23; 26:69-75; 27:62-66; 28:1-6;
Mark 15:46;
John 11:25,26; 18:15-18,25-27; 20:1-8,10-29; 21:15-19;
Acts 2:14-42;
1 Corinthians 15:3-8; 17-19

THE BIG IDEA

The truth and power of Jesus Christ's victory over sin and death is based on His resurrection.

AIMS OF THIS SESSION

During this session you will guide students to:
- Examine the biblical accounts of the resurrection of Jesus Christ;
- Discover the powerful facts of the resurrection of Jesus Christ;
- Implement a vital Christian lifestyle tied in with the knowledge and faith in the resurrected Christ.

WARM UP

SHARING THE GOOD NEWS OF THE RESURRECTION—

Students plan what to tell others about the Resurrection.

TEAM EFFORT— JUNIOR HIGH/ MIDDLE SCHOOL

THE TOMB REVISITED—

A skit with a modern day twist about the soldiers who guarded Jesus' tomb.

TEAM EFFORT— HIGH SCHOOL

VICTORY WORKSHEET—

How the resurrected Jesus can influence your life today.

IN THE WORD

THE RESURRECTION—

A Bible study on the evidence that the resurrection of Jesus Christ is an undeniable fact.

THINGS TO THINK ABOUT (OPTIONAL)

Questions to get students thinking and talking about the importance of the Resurrection to Christianity.

PARENT PAGE

A tool to get the session into the home and allow parents and young people to discuss how the Resurrection affects daily life.

LEADER'S DEVOTIONAL

"I know that my Redeemer lives, and that in the end he will stand upon the earth. And after my skin has been destroyed, yet in my flesh I will see God; I myself will see him with my own eyes—I, and not another. How my heart yearns within me!" (Job 19:25-27).

Life is a continuous series of unexpected surprises. You speed around town and never expect to get pulled over until the day when a motorcycle police officer nails you with his radar gun. You now expect to get a ticket, but the officer unexpectedly lets you off with a warning.

You do your best at work, but because of the economy, you know a raise is out of the question. Until your boss unexpectedly informs you one day that you'll be getting an increase in pay because of your hard work and productivity.

Little graces. The unexpected surprises that sprinkle life with spontaneity and joy. A note in the mail from a friend you haven't heard from in years. A colorful bunch of fresh cut flowers left at your door. Breakfast in bed. Little unexpected surprises remind us of God's generosity and grace. Unexpected surprises give us hope in the midst of a scary, chaotic world.

The resurrection of Jesus Christ is just the surprise we needed to bring us from sin, fear and insecurity into safety, forgiveness and wholeness before God. With more than a little grace, God showered the full extent of His love through a magnificent surprise that rocked the world. I guess you could say that the Resurrection was the beginning of God's surprise party in honor of Jesus. It is a celebration filled with laughter, joy and daily surprises. Your name is on the guest list, and Jesus can't wait for you to come.

As you get ready to teach this lesson, why not grab a few students and plan a surprise party for Jesus? The resurrection of Jesus is a perfect reason for a party. It will let all teenagers know that they're welcome at a party to which they never expected to be invited. (Written by Joey O'Connor.)

"I will never forget the day that I looked into the tomb. It changed my whole ministry. It came to me that my Savior was really alive, that His work on the cross for sinners so satisfied divine justice and divine character and divine righteousness, that I would never see my sins again. God raised Him from the dead as a guarantee to me personally that death has no more authority over the man in Christ. It has been shorn of its power...at the cross we see His love, but in the resurrection we see His power."—John Mitchell

THE RESURRECTION

KEY VERSES

"After the Sabbath, at dawn on the first day of the week, Mary Magdalene and the other Mary went to look at the tomb.

"There was a violent earthquake, for an angel of the Lord came down from heaven and, going to the tomb, rolled back the stone and sat on it. His appearance was like lightning, and his clothes were white as snow. The guards were so afraid of him that they shook and became like dead men.

"The angel said to the women, 'Do not be afraid, for I know that you are looking for Jesus, who was crucified. He is not here; he has risen, just as he said. Come and see the place where he lay.'" Matthew 28:1-6

BIBLICAL BASIS

Job 19:25-27; Matthew 16:21; 17:22,23; 26:69-75; 27:62-66; 28:1-6; Mark 15:46; John 11:25,26; 18:15-18,25-27; 20:1-8,10-29; 21:15-19; Acts 2:14-42; 1 Corinthians 15: 3-8;17-19

THE BIG IDEA

The truth and power of Jesus Christ's victory over sin and death is based on His resurrection.

WARM UP (5-10 MINUTES)

SHARING THE GOOD NEWS OF THE RESURRECTION

• Divide the students into groups of three or four.
• Give each group a copy of "Sharing the Good News of the Resurrection" on page 155 and a pen or pencil.
• Have each group complete the activity.
• As time permits, have groups share what they would say.
The resurrection of Jesus is the best news ever presented to humankind. Because of the Resurrection, we have life eternal and life abundant on earth.
Imagine for a moment that a very intelligent group of people from a remote part of the world has just been discovered. Your job as a group is to tell them about the resurrection of Jesus and what it means to their eternal lives. What would you say and how would you describe it to people who have never heard of Jesus?

After the resurrection of Jesus what did Peter proclaim, as recorded in Acts 2:14-37?

3. **Fact Three: The Resurrection is the only explanation for the empty tomb.**
Many people throughout history have tried to disprove the Resurrection. It is true that if the resurrection of Jesus can be disproved, then the cornerstone of the Christian faith would be destroyed.
What were the precautions taken, both by the friends of Jesus and by His enemies, to ensure that His body would not be stolen?
His enemies—Matthew 27:62-66

His enemies—Matthew 27:62-66

Listed below are the most common theories that skeptics throughout history have used to refute the Resurrection. Using the Scriptures you have looked at in this session so far, show the fallacy of these theories.

- The disciples stole and hid the body.
- The Roman or Jewish authorities took the body.
- Jesus never died. He walked out of the tomb.
- The women and the disciples went to the wrong tomb.
- The disciples simply hallucinated that they saw Jesus risen from the dead.

4. **Fact Four: The Resurrection is the reason for the beginning of the Christian Church and for its rapid growth.**
Within a very short period the Christian faith spread all over the Roman Empire and beyond. The disciples of Jesus always spoke of the resurrected and living Christ.
What was the main subject of Peter's sermon found in Acts 2:29-32?

What was the response of Peter's audience, according to Acts 2:37-42?

So What?
How does the reality of the Resurrection impact your life?

How will this week be different because of that impact?

THINGS TO THINK ABOUT (OPTIONAL)
• Use the questions on page 169 after or as apart of "In the Word."
1. How does the resurrection of Jesus separate Christianity from other religions?

2. Why do you think people deny Christianity even after hearing of the Resurrection?

3. If the Resurrection was a hoax, how would that affect your faith?

PARENT PAGE
• Distribute page to parents.

TEAM EFFORT—JUNIOR HIGH/ MIDDLE SCHOOL (15-20 Minutes)

THE TOMB REVISITED

• Have six students prepare "The Tomb Revisited" skit on pages 157-159 beforehand to present to the whole group. Discuss the events when they have finished the presentation.

TEAM EFFORT—HIGH SCHOOL (15-20 Minutes)

VICTORY WORKSHEET

• Give each student a copy of the "Victory Worksheet" on page 161 and a pen or pencil.
• Have students complete the activity by themselves.

After Jesus' resurrection, He appeared to several people, individually or in groups. Listed below are four of Jesus' personal appearances. After each example, answer the question that follows. These questions are intended for you to see how the resurrected Jesus can influence your life today.

1. Jesus appeared to Mary in her sorrow (John 20:10-18).
Question: What pain in your life can Jesus come and soothe?

2. Jesus appeared to the disciples in their fear (John 20:19-23).
Question: For what fears can Jesus give you confidence?

3. Jesus appeared to Peter after his denial (John 21:15-19; see also John 18:15-18, 25-27).
Question: In what ways have you "denied Christ?" Have you asked for Jesus' forgiveness?

4. Jesus appeared to Thomas in his doubts (John 20:24-29).
Question: What doubts or questions do you have that you need Christ to answer?

IN THE WORD (25-30 Minutes)

THE RESURRECTION

• Divide students into groups of three or four.
• Give each student a copy of "The Resurrection" on pages 163-167 and a pen or pencil, or display a copy using an overhead projector.
• Have students complete the Bible study.

I. The Event
"After the Sabbath, at dawn on the first day of the week, Mary Magdalene and the other Mary went to look at the tomb.

"There was a violent earthquake, for an angel of the Lord came down from heaven and, going to the tomb, rolled back the stone and sat on it. His appearance was like lightning, and his clothes were white as snow. The guards were so afraid of him that they shook and became like dead men.

"The angel said to the women, 'Do not be afraid, for I know that you are looking for Jesus, who was crucified. He is not here; he has risen, just as he said. Come and see the place where he lay'" (Matthew 28:1-6).

"Early on the first day of the week, while it was still dark, Mary Magdalene went to the tomb and saw that the stone had been removed from the entrance. So she came running to Simon Peter and the other disciple, the one Jesus loved, and said, 'They have taken the Lord out of the tomb, and we don't know where they have put him!'

"So Peter and the other disciple started for the tomb. Both were running, but the other disciple outran Peter and reached the tomb first. He bent over and looked in at the strips of linen lying there but did not go in. Then Simon Peter, who was behind him, arrived and went into the tomb. He saw the strips of linen lying there, as well as the burial cloth that had been around Jesus' head. The cloth was folded up by itself, separate from the linen. Finally the other disciple, who had reached the tomb first, also went inside. He saw and believed" (John 20:1-8).

Summarize these two passages in one sentence.

II. Looking at the Event
A. The Significance of the Resurrection of Jesus Christ
The most important event in human history is the resurrection of Jesus Christ. This single miracle has transformed the history of the world like no other. The Christian faith rests on the fact that Jesus Christ actually rose from the dead. Based upon this knowledge, we can be assured of the following:
– All He claimed about Himself must be true;
– All He said about life must be true;
– Our sins are forgiven. There is new life in the resurrection of Christ;
– Christians have eternal life, and will be resurrected from the dead just as Christ was.
What does Paul say about the Resurrection, in 1 Corinthians 15:17-19?

Since Jesus actually rose from the dead on the third day, what significance should that have for your faith?

What hope does the Resurrection give you personally?

Read John 11:25,26. How does Jesus' statement deal with the impact of the Resurrection on your life?

B. The Facts of the Resurrection
In order to believe in the resurrection of Jesus, you need not commit intellectual suicide. There are actually a number of facts that are unexplainable if Jesus did not actually rise from the dead. Let us explore these facts.

1. Fact One: Jesus foretold His resurrection.
Read Matthew 16:21 and Matthew 17:22,23. Why were the disciples distressed by the words of Jesus?

If Jesus did not rise from the dead on the third day, these verses from Matthew would make Him out to be a liar!

2. Fact Two: The testimony of eyewitnesses and the transformation of the disciples can be explained logically only by the resurrection appearance of Jesus. At the Crucifixion the followers of Jesus were in despair. Their hopes for a Messiah were crushed. Yet after three days their lives were transformed.
Read 1 Corinthians 15:3-8. List those to whom Jesus appeared after He was raised from the dead.

There is no doubt that the disciples' lives were changed after Jesus' resurrection appearances. According to Matthew 26:69-75, what did Peter do immediately before the Resurrection?

SHARING THE GOOD NEWS OF THE RESURRECTION

The resurrection of Jesus is the best news ever presented to humankind. Because of the Resurrection, we have life eternal and life abundant on earth.

Imagine for a moment that a very intelligent group of people from a remote part of the earth has just been discovered. Your job as a group is to tell them about the resurrection of Jesus and what it means to their eternal lives. What would you say and how would you describe it to people who have never heard of Jesus?

....

....

....

....

TEAM EFFORT

THE TOMB REVISITED[1]

Setting: Four guards are sleeping in front of the tomb of Jesus. They are snoring and they awaken without paying any attention to the tomb.

Scene I

Louie: (Wakes up, rubs eyes, yawns and stretches) Man is it cold out here—I better build a fire. (Begins to rub two sticks, and to put wood and leaves together, blows into it, etc.)

Bernie: Hey, wat'cha doing Louie?

Louie: Oh, just putting my Boy Scout training to use.

Bernie: Forgot the matches again, eh? (Gets up and goes over to a knapsack and finds a box of matches.) Here ya go. (Throws matches to Louie.)

Marvin: (Awakening from sleep) Hey what's going on with all the noise?

Louie: (testily) I'm trying to get a fire going for breakfast.

Marvin: Never mind for me—I've got mine all ready to go. (Shows a box of cereal and begins to prepare his own breakfast.)

Norman: (Who by this time has also awakened—sniffs in the air as if something is burning.) Hey what's burning?

Louie: Probably wood.

Norman: (Walking toward fire) No, no. It smells like something rotten is burning. (Pause)

Bernie: Oh it's just your imagination.

Marvin: No—I smell something now too.

Louie: What's that in the fire there (Pokes a stick in the "fire" and pulls out a burned shoe.)

Norman: Those are my new Adidas you've been using for kindling wood, you idiot. Why I ought to strangle you with my bare...(This last line is said while chasing Louie around the fire. Louie falls at Norman's knees, wraps his arms around him and begs for mercy.)

Louie: Please, Norman—have mercy on me.

Bernie & Marvin: Yeah Norman, give him a break. (Just then Norman notices the empty tomb—His eyes bug out and he says:)

Norman: Look! The tomb! It's empty!

Everyone: We're in big trouble.

Marvin: We are all gonna get fired.

Louie: (crying) I'm going to lose my pension—and I only had three more years to go until retirement.

Bernie: Don't feel bad, I've got a house to pay for and a son attending Jerusalem State Medical School.

Norman: What are you guys talking about. It's not our fault that the tomb is empty. Jesus must have really come back from the dead—just as He predicted.

Louie: What makes you say that, Norman?

Norman: Well, that rock. It's moved. Who do you think moved it—the tooth fairy?

Marvin: (glaring at Bernie) I'm sure we would have slept through an earthquake.

Bernie: Well, don't look at me—I don't know where Jesus is.

TEAM EFFORT

Louie: Well, if it's not our fault that He's gone, let's get down to headquarters and tell the chief priests to put out an APB.

Everyone: Right! (Pick up sleeping bags, put out fire, etc. as curtain closes.)

Scene II

Setting: A room with a desk and chairs, depicting the place of the chief priests.

Chief Priest Caiaphas: (excitedly) What are you guys doing here—you're supposed to be at the tomb!

Louie: (nonchalantly) There's nothing there to guard. Jesus is gone.

Chief Priest Annas: (very excitedly) Gone! Where did He go?!

Marvin: Norman thinks that Jesus has risen from the dead—just like He predicted He would.

Annas: (to all) You nincompoops! We can't have people believing Jesus came back from the dead. Think what it will do to our religion and more importantly—all of our jobs! Why—who is going to give to the Temple if they think there is a risen savior?

Bernie: Well, what do you want us to do?

Caiaphas: (coming back to the guards) Look. Who else knows about Jesus rising from the dead? All the guards: Nobody.

Caiaphas: (rubbing his hands together) All right, this is what we are going to say to the press. Quote: "We do not know the whereabouts of Jesus of Nazareth's body—because while the guards were sleeping, His disciples stole Him away."

Norman: That's no good. If we were sleeping, how would we know His disciples stole the body?

Annas: (testily) Look, Norman, we are doing this for you as well as ourselves. This statement will not only save your job but will also make you rich.

Norman: (sarcastically) How?

Annas: (pulls out a wad of money) This money is for you—if you can keep our little secret. Do I have any takers, boys?

Bernie: (greedily stuffs money in pockets) I've got a boy in medical school.

Louie: I need a little extra for my retirement. (Stuffing money into his pockets.)

Marvin: Everybody likes money.

Norman: (firmly) Money never brought a man back from the dead, though. (Exits right leaving the others standing in the room with a dumb look on their faces.)

Note:

1. Bill Calvin, *Ideas Numbers 21-24* (El Cajon, Calif.: Youth Specialties, 1984), pp. 182-184. Used by permission.

THE RESURRECTION

VICTORY WORKSHEET[1]

After Jesus' resurrection, He appeared to several people, individually or in groups. Listed below are four of Jesus' personal appearances. After each example, answer the question that follows. These questions are intended for you to see how the resurrected Jesus can influence your life today.

1. Jesus appeared to Mary in her sorrow (John 20:10-18).

Question: What pain in your life can Jesus come and soothe?

....

....

2. Jesus appeared to the disciples in their fear (John 20:19-23).

Question: For what fears can Jesus give you confidence?

....

....

3. Jesus appeared to Peter after his denial (John 21:15-19; see also John 18:15-18, 25-27)

Question: In what ways have you "denied Christ?" Have you asked for Jesus' forgiveness?

....

....

4. Jesus appeared to Thomas in his doubts (John 20:24-29).

Question: What doubts or questions do you have that you need Christ to answer?

....

....

Note:

1. A Bible study by Doug Fields, Saddleback Valley Community Church, Mission Viejo, Calif., 1995.

 **IN THE WORD**

THE RESURRECTION

I. The Event

"After the Sabbath, at dawn on the first day of the week, Mary Magdalene and the other Mary went to look at the tomb.

"There was a violent earthquake, for an angel of the Lord came down from heaven and, going to the tomb, rolled back the stone and sat on it. His appearance was like lightning, and his clothes were white as snow. The guards were so afraid of him that they shook and became like dead men.

"The angel said to the women, 'Do not be afraid, for I know that you are looking for Jesus, who was crucified. He is not here; he has risen, just as he said. Come and see the place where he lay'" (Matthew 28:1-6).

"Early on the first day of the week, while it was still dark, Mary Magdalene went to the tomb and saw that the stone had been removed from the entrance. So she came running to Simon Peter and the other disciple, the one Jesus loved, and said, 'They have taken the Lord out of the tomb, and we don't know where they have put him!'

"So Peter and the other disciple started for the tomb. Both were running, but the other disciple outran Peter and reached the tomb first. He bent over and looked in at the strips of linen lying there but did not go in. Then Simon Peter, who was behind him, arrived and went into the tomb. He saw the strips of linen lying there, as well as the burial cloth that had been around Jesus' head. The cloth was folded up by itself, separate from the linen. Finally the other disciple, who had reached the tomb first, also went inside. He saw and believed" (John 20:1-8).

Summarize these two passages in one sentence.

....

II. Looking at the Event

A.   The Significance of the Resurrection of Jesus Christ

The most important event in human history is the resurrection of Jesus Christ. This single miracle has transformed the history of the world like no other.

The Christian faith rests on the fact that Jesus Christ actually rose from the dead. Based upon this knowledge, we can be assured of the following:

- All He claimed about Himself must be true;
- All He said about life must be true;
- Our sins are forgiven. There is new life in the resurrection of Christ;
- Christians have eternal life, and will be resurrected from the dead just as Christ was.

What does Paul say about the Resurrection, in 1 Corinthians 15:17-19?

....

....

Since Jesus actually rose from the dead on the third day, what significance should that have for your faith?

....

....

IN THE WORD

What hope does the Resurrection give you personally?

....

....

Read John 11:25,26. How does Jesus' statement deal with the impact of the Resurrection on your life?

....

....

B. The Facts of the Resurrection
In order to believe in the resurrection of Jesus, you need not commit intellectual suicide. There are actually a number of facts that are unexplainable if Jesus did not actually rise from the dead. Let us explore these facts.
1. Fact One: Jesus foretold His resurrection.

Read Matthew 16:21 and Matthew 17:22,23. Why were the disciples distressed by the words of Jesus?

....

If Jesus did not rise from the dead on the third day, these verses from Matthew would make Him out to be a liar!
2. Fact Two: The testimony of eyewitnesses and the transformation of the disciples can be explained logically only by the resurrection appearances of Jesus.
At the Crucifixion the followers of Jesus were in despair. Their hopes for a Messiah were crushed. Yet after three days their lives were transformed.

Read 1 Corinthians 15:3-8. List those to whom Jesus appeared after He was raised from the dead.

....

....

There is no doubt that the disciples' lives were changed after Jesus' Resurrection appearances. According to Matthew 26:69-75, what did Peter do immediately before the Resurrection?

....

....

After the resurrection of Jesus what did Peter proclaim, as recorded in Acts 2:14-37?

....

....

3. Fact Three: The Resurrection is the only explanation for the empty tomb.
Many people throughout history have tried to disprove the Resurrection. It is true that if the resurrection of Jesus can be disproved, then the cornerstone of the Christian faith would be destroyed.
What were the precautions taken, both by the friends of Jesus and by His enemies, to ensure that His body would not be stolen?

IN THE WORD

THE RESURRECTION

His friends—Mark 15:46 ....

....

....

His enemies—Matthew 27:62-66 ....

....

....

Listed below are the most common theories that skeptics throughout history have used to refute the Resurrection. Using the Scriptures you have looked at in this session so far, show the fallacy of these theories.

• **The disciples stole and hid the body.**

....

• **The Roman or Jewish authorities took the body.**

....

• **Jesus never died. He walked out of the tomb.**

....

• **The women and the disciples went to the wrong tomb.**

....

• **The disciples simply hallucinated that they saw Jesus risen from the dead.**

....

4. Fact Four: The Resurrection is the reason for the beginning of the Christian Church and for its rapid growth.
   Within a very short time period the Christian faith spread all over the Roman Empire and beyond. The disciples of Jesus always spoke of the resurrected and living Christ.

What was the main subject of Peter's sermon found in Acts 2:29-32?

....

....

What was the response of Peter's audience, according to Acts 2:37-42?

....

....

THE RESURRECTION

SO WHAT?

How does the reality of the Resurrection impact your life?

....

....

....

How will this week be different because of that impact?

....

....

....

THINGS TO THINK ABOUT

1. How does the resurrection of Jesus separate Christianity from other religions?

....

....

....

2. Why do you think people deny Christianity even after hearing of the Resurrection?

....

....

....

3. If the Resurrection was a hoax, how would that affect your faith?

....

....

⬤ PARENT PAGE

THE RESURRECTION AND YOU

As Christians, we have the power of the Resurrection living in us. Because of the resurrection of Jesus, you can have hope for today and for eternity.

According to 1 Corinthians 15:17-19, how important is the resurrection of Jesus Christ?

....

....

How can the resurrection of Jesus affect your life today?

....

....

What will you do differently because you know the power of His resurrection?

....

....

How can you use the resurrection power of Jesus to help your family live out the Christian life?

....

....

....

Session 10 "The Resurrection"
Date...

THE ASCENSION OF JESUS

KEY VERSES

"In my former book, Theophilus, I wrote about all that Jesus began to do and to teach until the day he was taken up to heaven, after giving instructions through the Holy Spirit to the apostles he had chosen. After his suffering, he showed himself to these men and gave many convincing proofs that he was alive. He appeared to them over a period of forty days and spoke about the kingdom of God. On one occasion, while he was eating with them, he gave them this command: 'Do not leave Jerusalem, but wait for the gift my Father promised, which you have heard me speak about. For John baptized with water, but in a few days you will be baptized with the Holy Spirit.'" Acts 1:1-5

BIBLICAL BASIS

Matthew 4:19;
Mark 16:19,20;
Luke 24:50-53;
John 14:1-3; 15:1-11;
Acts 1:1-11;
Romans 8:34;
Galatians 6:9,10;
Colossians 3:1

THE BIG IDEA

The Ascension was Christ's glorified departure from His earthly life that allowed the coming of the Holy Spirit and the beginning of Christ's church on earth.

AIMS OF THIS SESSION

During this session you will guide students to:
• Examine the hope of the ascension of Jesus Christ;
• Discover the principles of power and proclamation of the Christian faith;
• Implement a desire to receive the same power of the Holy Spirit promised by Jesus in order to proclaim His good news.

WARM UP

EASTER MEMORIES—
Students share memories with one another.

TEAM EFFORT— JUNIOR HIGH/ MIDDLE SCHOOL

THE INCOMPARABLE CHRIST—
Examples of Christ's power and presence.

TEAM EFFORT— HIGH SCHOOL

ABIDING IN CHRIST AND YOU—
An understanding of what abiding in Christ means.

IN THE WORD

THE ASCENSION OF JESUS—
A Bible study on the effects of Jesus' ascension on the world and on His followers.

THINGS TO THINK ABOUT (OPTIONAL)

Questions to get students thinking and talking about the importance of the Ascension to their personal lives.

PARENT PAGE

A tool to get the session into the home and allow parents and young people to discuss the ascension of Christ.

LEADER'S DEVOTIONAL

"Let us not become weary in doing good, for at the proper time we will reap a harvest if we do not give up. Therefore, as we have opportunity, let us do good to all people, especially to those who belong to the family of believers" (Galatians 6:9,10).

I am really grateful for the family I grew up in. Like any other family, my family isn't a perfect family. The Cleavers we are not, but we sure are a good family. My mom and dad had seven screaming, rambunctious children and I was number five. Two boys... five girls. My brother, Neil, and I were definitely outnumbered. Growing up, we all had our fair share of fights and arguments, but despite all this, we are still a good family. My parents never got separated or divorced. In fact, many of the values and character qualities I learned from my folks are the same things I'm teaching my two little girls right now.

When I think about the home environment I grew up in and then contrast that with the home lives of many of these students I've worked with, I'm amazed at God's blessing in my life. There are so many young people today whose anger, bitterness and rebellion from God is rooted in what's happening at home. When you look at the students in your ministry who have troubled home lives, don't you just wish you could give them warm and secure homes to live in? How many problems and struggles could be prevented if these students lived in homes filled with love?

Short of taking legal action, you and I both know it's almost impossible to shield our students from the damage done in abusive homes. The one hope, the most valuable gift we could give them, is the promises of Jesus found in this lesson. Jesus' ascension and the promise of His abiding presence in our lives can give students a firm foundation for their lives. Jesus' presence and the extended family of God can give them the warm sense of security, comfort and community they don't find at home. You have the remarkable opportunity to show teenagers how to belong to and create loving families of their own someday. (Written by Joey O'Connor.)

"The power of the Resurrection is the power of personal regeneration. Resurrection always spells regeneration. The two things must always be kept together: the new world and the new person. Resurrection is not just a passport to heaven, but a power to change us now."—Lloyd Ogilvie

THE ASCENSION OF JESUS

KEY VERSES

"In my former book, Theophilus, I wrote about all that Jesus began to do and to teach until the day he was taken up to heaven, after giving instructions through the Holy Spirit to the apostles he had chosen. After his suffering, he showed himself to these men and gave many convincing proofs that he was alive. He appeared to them over a period of forty days and spoke about the kingdom of God. On one occasion, while he was eating with them, he gave them this command: 'Do not leave Jerusalem, but wait for the gift my Father promised, which you have heard me speak about. For John baptized with water, but in a few days you will be baptized with the Holy Spirit.'" Acts 1:1-5

BIBLICAL BASIS

Matthew 4:19; Mark 16:19,20; Luke 24:50-53; John 14:1-3; 15:1-11; Acts 1:1-11; Romans 8:34; Galatians 6:9,10; Colossians 3:1

THE BIG IDEA

The Ascension was Christ's glorified departure from His earthly life that allowed the coming of the Holy Spirit and the beginning of Christ's church on earth.

WARM UP (5-10 MINUTES)

EASTER MEMORIES

• Divide students into pairs and have them share:
   An early childhood memory about Easter;
   A meaningful Easter memory;
   Reasons to celebrate Easter.

TEAM EFFORT—JUNIOR HIGH/MIDDLE SCHOOL (15-20 MINUTES)

THE INCOMPARABLE CHRIST

• Give each student a copy of "The Incomparable Christ" on page 177.
• Have volunteers take turns reading parts of the article aloud.

Fold

175

What event is described and what promise is given in verses 9-11?

II. Looking at the Event

What took place before the ascension of Jesus, according to Acts 1:1-5?

What promise did the two men in white robes give to the disciples in Acts 1:10,11?

What is the significance of this promise?

Where did Christ go after the Ascension? Read Mark 16:19 and Colossians 3:1.

What is Christ doing in heaven? Read John 14:1-3 and Romans 8:34.

III. The Ascension and You

The disciples had seen Jesus work miracles. They had observed the agony of His death and the joy and confusion of His resurrection. Now, after 40 days on earth in His resurrected body, Jesus ascended into heaven, where He would sit at the right hand of God, and the disciples watched, amazed and stunned, as He disappeared into the sky. After the Ascension, the disciples were transformed people.

Our response in the twentieth century should be the same response as the disciples had in A.D. 33.

A. Joy and Worship

Read Luke 24:50-53. What was the response of the disciples after Jesus ascended into heaven?

How can this study of Jesus Christ cause you to have deeply rooted joy and a new sense of appreciation as you worship God?

What steps can you take to make joy and worship a greater part of your life?

B. Power

What did Jesus tell His disciples in Acts 1:8 about power?

What kind of power is He talking about in this verse?

How would this power help your life?

What steps can you take to empower your life with the Holy Spirit?

C. Proclamation

According to Mark 16:19,20, what did the disciples do when Jesus was taken up to heaven?

The word "proclamation" means to announce, tell or preach. The disciples proclaimed everywhere the Resurrection and the new life available in Jesus.

How do you think joy, worship and power relate to proclaiming the good news of Christ?

So What?

Who do you know who needs the good news of Jesus Christ proclaimed to them?

What steps will you take to share that news?

When will you take the first step?

THINGS TO THINK ABOUT (OPTIONAL)

• Use the questions on page 187 after or as a part of "In the Word."

1. What is the significance of the Ascension?

2. How would you have felt if you had seen Jesus ascend into heaven?

3. What is the relationship between the ascension of Christ and the promise of Acts 1:8?

PARENT PAGE

• Distribute page to parents.

After reading this incredible piece about Christ, brainstorm other illustrations of Christ's presence and power since His ascension to heaven.

"More than 1,900 years ago there was a Man born contrary to the laws of life. This Man lived in poverty and was reared in obscurity. He did not travel extensively. Only once did He cross the boundary of the country in which He lived; that was during His exile in childhood. He possessed neither wealth nor influence. His relatives were inconspicuous and had neither training nor formal education. In infancy He startled a king; in childhood He puzzled doctors; in manhood He ruled the course of nature, walked upon the billows as if pavements, and hushed the sea to sleep. He healed the multitudes without medicine and made no charge for His service. He never wrote a song, and yet He has furnished the theme for more songs than all the songwriters combined. He never founded a college, but all the schools put together cannot boast of having as many students. He never marshaled an army, nor drafted a soldier, nor fired a gun; and yet no leader ever had more volunteers who have, under His orders, made more rebels stack arms and surrender without a shot fired. He never practiced medicine, and yet He has healed more broken hearts than all the doctors far and near. Every seventh day the wheels of commerce cease their turning and multitudes wend their way to worshiping assemblies to pay homage and respect to Him. The names of the past proud statesmen of Greece and Rome have come and gone. The names of the past scientists, philosophers and theologians have come and gone, but the name of this Man abounds more and more. Though time has spread 1,900 years between the people of this generation and the scene of His crucifixion, yet He still lives. Herod could not destroy Him, and the grave could not hold Him. He stands forth upon the highest pinnacle of heavenly glory, proclaimed of God, acknowledged by angels, adored by saints and feared by devils, as the living personal Christ, our Lord and Savior." —Author Unknown

TEAM EFFORT—HIGH SCHOOL (15-20 Minutes)

ABIDING IN CHRIST AND YOU

- Give each student a copy of "Abiding in Christ and You" on page 179 and a pen or pencil, or display a copy using an overhead projector.
- Complete the page as a group except for the last two questions. Have each student spend a quiet minute or two alone to answer these last two questions.

When Christ ascended into heaven, we were told we could still follow Him even while on earth. To better understand this concept, let's look at the principle of abiding in Christ: To follow Christ means to keep in contact with Him. If you lose contact, the chances are that weakness will overcome you. Your ability to abide in Christ lies in continual contact with the strength and power of Christ.

William Barclay said this about abiding in Christ: "It will mean arranging life, arranging prayer, arranging silence in such a way that there is never a day when we give ourselves a chance to forget him."

Read John 15:1-11. Listed below are six results of abiding in Christ.

1. Having Prayers Answered.

What principles for prayer do you see in John 15:7?

2. Glorifying God.
According to John 15:8, how do we glorify God?

---

3. Becoming Christ's Disciple.
How do we show ourselves to be Christ's disciples according to John 15:8?

Read Matthew 4:19. What does it take to become a disciple?

4. Remaining in Christ's Love.
How do we remain (abide) in His love as shown in John 15:9,10?

5. Having Your Joy Completed.
According to John 15:11, what is the key result of abiding in Christ?

Now that you have studied the results of abiding in Christ, what is your response?

6. Bearing Eternal Fruit.
Your job as a branch is not to worry and struggle to bear fruit. Your job as a branch is to abide in the vine. Fruit is the natural result of abiding. After reading this entire section of Scripture, what do you see as a fruitful life?

What would it take for you to give all that you are to Christ?

IN THE WORD (25-30 Minutes)

THE ASCENSION OF JESUS

- Divide students into groups of three or four.
- Give each student a copy of "The Ascension of Jesus" on pages 181-185 and a pen or pencil, or display a copy using an overhead projector.
- Have students complete the Bible study.

1. The Event

"So when they met together, they asked him, 'Lord, are you at this time going to restore the kingdom to Israel?'

"He said to them: 'It is not for you to know the times or dates the Father has set by his own authority. But you will receive power when the Holy Spirit comes on you; and you will be my witnesses in Jerusalem, and in all Judea and Samaria, and to the ends of the earth.'

"After he said this, he was taken up before their very eyes, and a cloud hid him from their sight.

"They were looking intently up into the sky as he was going, when suddenly two men dressed in white stood beside them. 'Men of Galilee,' they said, 'why do you stand here looking into the sky? This same Jesus, who has been taken from you into heaven, will come back in the same way you have seen him go into heaven'" (Acts 1:6-11).

How did Jesus respond to the disciples' question in verse 6?

What is the vital importance of verse 8?

Fold

TEAM EFFORT

THE INCOMPARABLE CHRIST

After reading this incredible piece about Christ, brainstorm other illustrations of Christ's presence and power since His ascension to heaven.

"More than 1,900 years ago there was a Man born contrary to the laws of life. This Man lived in poverty and was reared in obscurity. He did not travel extensively. Only once did He cross the boundary of the country in which He lived; that was during His exile in childhood. He possessed neither wealth nor influence. His relatives were inconspicuous and had neither training nor formal education. In infancy He startled a king; in childhood He puzzled doctors; in manhood He ruled the course of nature, walked upon the billows as if pavements, and hushed the sea to sleep. He healed the multitudes without medicine and made no charge for His service. He never wrote a book, yet all the libraries of the world could not hold the books that have been written about Him. He never wrote a song, and yet He has furnished the theme for more songs than all the songwriters combined. He never founded a college, but all the schools put together cannot boast of having as many students. He never marshaled an army, nor drafted a soldier, nor fired a gun; and yet no leader ever had more volunteers who have, under His orders, made more rebels stack arms and surrender without a shot fired. He never practiced medicine, and yet He has healed more broken hearts than all the doctors far and near. Every seventh day the wheels of commerce cease their turning and multitudes wend their way to worshiping assemblies to pay homage and respect to Him. The names of the past proud statesmen of Greece and Rome have come and gone. The names of the past scientists, philosophers and theologians have come and gone, but the name of this Man abounds more and more. Though time has spread 1,900 years between the people of this generation and the scene of His crucifixion, yet He still lives. Herod could not destroy Him and the grave could not hold Him. He stands forth upon the highest pinnacle of heavenly glory, proclaimed of God, acknowledged by angels, adored by saints and feared by devils, as the living personal Christ, our Lord and Savior." —Author Unknown

THE ASCENSION OF JESUS

TEAM EFFORT

ABIDING IN CHRIST AND YOU

When Christ ascended into heaven, we were told we could still follow Him even while on earth. To better understand this concept, let's look at the principle of abiding in Christ: To follow Christ means to keep in contact with Him. If you lose contact, the chances are that weakness will overcome you. Your ability to abide in Christ lies in continual contact with the strength and power of Christ.

William Barclay said this about abiding in Christ: "It will mean arranging life, arranging prayer, arranging silence in such a way that there is never a day when we give ourselves a chance to forget him."[1]

Read John 15:1-11.

Listed below are six results of abiding in Christ.

1. Having Prayer Answered.

What principles for prayer do you see in John 15:7?

....

2. Glorifying God.

According to John 15:8, how do we glorify God?

....

....

3. Becoming Christ's Disciple.

How do we show ourselves to be Christ's disciples according to John 15:8?

....

....

Read Matthew 4:19. What does it take to become a disciple?

....

....

4. Remaining in Christ's Love.

How do we remain (abide) in His love as shown in John 15:9,10?

....

....

5. Having Your Joy Be Completed.

According to John 15:11, what is the key result of abiding in Christ?

....

....

6. Bearing Eternal Fruit.

Your job as a branch is not to worry and struggle to bear fruit. Your job as a branch is to abide in the vine. Fruit is the natural result of abiding. After reading this entire section of Scripture, what do you see as a fruitful life?

....

....

....

Now that you have studied the results of abiding in Christ, what is your response?

....

....

....

What would it take for you to give all that you are to Christ?

....

....

....

Note:

1. William Barclay, *The Gospel of John, Vol. II, The Daily Study Bible Series* (Philadelphia, Penn.: Westminster Press, 1975), p. 176.

THE ASCENSION OF JESUS

IN THE WORD

THE ASCENSION OF JESUS

I. The Event

"So when they met together, they asked him, 'Lord, are you at this time going to restore the kingdom to Israel?'

"He said to them: 'It is not for you to know the times or dates the Father has set by his own authority. But you will receive power when the Holy Spirit comes on you; and you will be my witnesses in Jerusalem, and in all Judea and Samaria, and to the ends of the earth.'

"After he said this, he was taken up before their very eyes, and a cloud hid him from their sight.

"They were looking intently up into the sky as he was going, when suddenly two men dressed in white stood beside them. 'Men of Galilee,' they said, 'why do you stand here looking into the sky? This same Jesus, who has been taken from you into heaven, will come back in the same way you have seen him go into heaven'" (Acts 1.6-11).

How did Jesus respond to the disciples' question in verse 6?

....

....

What is the vital importance of verse 8?

....

....

What event is described and what promise is given in verses 9-11?

....

....

II. Looking at the Event

What took place before the ascension of Jesus, according to Acts 1:1-5?

....

....

What promise did the two men in white robes give to the disciples in Acts 1:10,11?

....

....

What is the significance of this promise?

....

....

Where did Christ go after the Ascension? Read Mark 16:19 and Colossians 3:1.

....

 **IN THE WORD**

What is Christ doing in heaven? Read John 14:1-3 and Romans 8:34.

....

....

III. The Ascension and You

The disciples had seen Jesus work miracles. They had observed the agony of His death and the joy and confusion of His resurrection. Now, after 40 days on earth in His resurrected body, Jesus ascended into heaven, where He would sit at the right hand of God, and the disciples watched, amazed and stunned, as He disappeared into the sky. After the Ascension, the disciples were transformed people.

Our response in the twentieth century should be the same response as the disciples had in A.D. 33.

A. Joy and worship

Read Luke 24:50-53. What was the response of the disciples after Jesus ascended into heaven?

....

How can this study of Jesus Christ cause you to have deeply rooted joy and a new sense of appreciation as you worship God?

....

What steps can you take to make joy and worship a greater part of your life?

....

B. Power

What did Jesus tell His disciples in Acts 1:8 about power?

....

What kind of power is He talking about in this verse?

....

How would this power help your life?

....

What steps can you take to empower your life with the Holy Spirit?

....

C. Proclamation

According to Mark 16:19,20, what did the disciples do when Jesus was taken up to heaven?

....

....

THE ASCENSION OF
JESUS

N THE WORD

The word "proclamation" means to announce, tell or preach. The disciples proclaimed everywhere the Resurrection and the new life available in Jesus.

How do you think joy, worship and power relate to proclaiming the good news of Christ?

....

....

So What?

Who do you who know needs the good news of Jesus Christ proclaimed to them?

....

What steps will you take to share that news?

....

When will you take the first step?

....

....

THINGS TO THINK ABOUT

1. What is the significance of the Ascension?

....

....

2. How would you have felt if you had seen Jesus ascend into heaven?

....

....

3. What is the relationship between the ascension of Christ and the promise of Acts 1:8?

....

....

....

THE ASCENSION OF JESUS

PARENT PAGE

THE ASCENSION: AN INDUCTIVE BIBLE STUDY

Read together Acts 1:1-11 and answer as many of these questions from this Bible study as you possible can.

1. Who?
What persons are involved in this Scripture?

....

Who wrote it?

....

Who is it written to and about?

....

Who does it refer to or mention?

....

2. What?
What is taking place?

....

What words are repeated, omitted or emphasized?

....

What action should be taken as a result?

....

What can you learn about God, Christ and the Holy Spirit from these Scriptures?

....

3. Where?
Where is it happening?

....

What places are referred to?

....

4. When?
What time of day, year, etc.?

....

How long after Christ was crucified did this occur?

....

5. Why?
What reasons, if any, are given for Christ's ascension?

....

6. How?
How are we to live according to this passage?

....
....
....

7. Application
How does this passage affect our lives?

....
....
....

Session 11 "The Ascension of Jesus"
Date ....

THE SECOND COMING

Key VERSES

"As Jesus was sitting on the Mount of Olives, the disciples came to him privately. 'Tell us,' they said, 'when will this happen, and what will be the sign of your coming and of the end of the age?'

"Jesus answered: 'Watch out that no one deceives you. For many will come in my name, claiming, "I am the Christ," and will deceive many. You will hear of wars and rumors of wars, but see to it that you are not alarmed. Such things must happen, but the end is still to come. Nation will rise against nation, and kingdom against kingdom. There will be famines and earthquakes in various places. All these are the beginning of birth pains.'" Matthew 24:3-8

Biblical Basis

Proverbs 3:5,6;
Isaiah 40:29-31;
Micah 6:8;
Matthew 16:24; 24:1-51;
Luke 10:27; 12:35-48;
John 15:1-11;
Romans 12:1,2;
1 Thessalonians 5:1-11;
Titus 2:13;
Revelation 22:20,21

The Big Idea

The second coming of Christ, preceded by chaotic times on earth, will be filled with the power and glory of God. Christians are to live faithfully each day to prepare for His return.

Aims of This Session

During this session you will guide students to:
• Examine the interesting facts surrounding the second coming of Christ;
• Discover what Christians can do to prepare and watch for the return of Christ to earth;
• Implement a faithfulness to live each day as if Christ could be returning at any time.

Warm Up

The Message—
Students develop a slogan to tell the world of Christ's return.

Team Effort— Junior High/ Middle School

Abiding in Christ—
A look at what abiding in Christ means.

Team Effort— High School

What Would You Do?—
Students share what they would do if they knew when Christ would return.

In the Word

The Second Coming of Christ—
A Bible study on Christ's return to earth.

Things to Think About (OPTIONAL)

Questions to get students thinking and talking about their feelings and concerns about the future.

Parent Page

A tool to get the session into the home and allow parents and young people to discuss how to respond to the promise of Christ's return.

LEADER'S DEVOTIONAL

"He who testifies to these things says, 'Yes, I am coming soon.' Amen. Come, Lord Jesus. The grace of the Lord Jesus be with God's people. Amen" (Revelation 22:20,21).

A few years ago I attended a youth worker's conference in which a fellow youth worker shared with me a simple list of qualities he looked for in students who wanted to serve on his student ministry team. He looked for students who were faithful, available and teachable.

Ever since that conversation years ago, I've used that same list of character qualities to disciple and develop students on my student ministry team. I also use these qualities as a filter for my own life to make sure I'm growing in my relationship with God as well.

When we study the second coming of Christ, only by being faithful to God will we be ready for Jesus' return. If we make ourselves available to the Holy Spirit every day, we will be prepared to meet Jesus with eager anticipation. If we remain teachable with open hearts ready to receive God's correction and instruction, we will remind ourselves of our temporary residence here on planet earth.

Whether you're a full-time, part-time or volunteer youth worker, God isn't only interested in seeing these qualities developed in students' lives; He wants you to be faithful. He wants you to be available. And He wants you to be teachable. The same qualities we desire to develop in the lives of teenagers are the very same ones God wants to create in our lives. As youth workers, we are co-learners, co-followers and co-disciples with our students. The only thing that separates us from them is age and experience. We all follow the same Lord. Each one of us must individually prepare for the return of Christ. Staying faithful, available and teachable will keep our eyes on the sky and not on earth. (Written by Joey O'Connor.)

"Because we do not know the day or the hour of our Lord's return, we must constantly be ready. The believer who starts to neglect the 'blessed hope' (Titus 2:13) will gradually develop a cold heart, a worldly attitude, and an unfaithful life (Luke 12:35-48)."
—Warren Wiersbe

Tear along perforation. Fold and place this bible *Tuck-in* ™ in your Bible for session use.

THE SECOND COMING

KEY VERSES

"As Jesus was sitting on the Mount of Olives, the disciples came to him privately. 'Tell us,' they said, 'when will this happen, and what will be the sign of your coming and of the end of the age?'

"Jesus answered: 'Watch out that no one deceives you. For many will come in my name, claiming, "I am the Christ," and will deceive many. You will hear of wars and rumors of wars, but see to it that you are not alarmed. Such things must happen, but the end is still to come. Nation will rise against nation, and kingdom against kingdom. There will be famines and earthquakes in various places. All these are the beginning of birth pains.'" Matthew 24:3-8

BIBLICAL BASIS

Proverbs 3:5,6; Isaiah 40:29-31; Micah 6:8; Matthew 16:24; 24:1-51; Luke 10:27; 12:35-43; John 15:1-11; Romans 12:1,2; 1 Thessalonians 5:1-11; Titus 2:13; Revelation 22:20,21

THE BIG IDEA

The second coming of Christ, preceded by chaotic times on earth, will be filled with the power and glory of God. Christians are to live faithfully each day to prepare for His return.

WARM UP (5-10 Minutes)

THE MESSAGE

- Divide students into groups of three or four.
- Give each group a piece of paper and a felt-tip pen.
- Tell the students "You have five minutes to come up with a phrase (a message) that will be written in the sky for every human being to read in order to prepare them for the immediate return of Jesus Christ. As a group, come up with what that simple, but important phrase, will be."
- Have students share their messages.

B. Watchfulness.

"To live without watchfulness invites disaster. A thief does not send a letter saying when he is going to burgle a house; his principal weapon in his nefarious undertakings is surprise; therefore a householder who has valuables in his house must maintain a constant guard. But to get this picture right, we must remember that the watchdog of the Christian for the coming of Christ is not that of terror-stricken fear and shivering apprehension; it is the watching in eager expectation for the coming of glory and joy."

What does it mean in practical terms to have an attitude of watchfulness?

Read 1 Thessalonians 5:1-11. How will the Lord come (see v. 2)?

List the suggestions found in verses 4-11 that will help you prepare for the coming of the Lord. Which of the listed suggestions do you need to work on the most? Circle your answer. What specifically will you do to work on this area of your Christian life?

C. Faithfulness.

Faithfulness is one of the key ingredients in living a consistent Christian life. The Scripture tells us that the rewards of faithfulness are great. What is the reward for the faithful servant in the parable found in Matthew 24:45-51? What is the reward for the unfaithful servant?

On the scale below, place a mark indicating your general level of faithfulness to God.

Faithfulness

1	2	3	4	5	6	7	8	9	10
Never faithful		Seldom faithful		Sometimes faithful		Usually faithful			Always faithful

So What?

What will you do to improve your level of faithfulness?

THINGS TO THINK ABOUT (OPTIONAL)

- Use the questions on page 205 after or as a part of "In the Word."

1. Do you think our world is getting better or worse with each generation? Why?

2. What are your greatest fears about the future?

3. Why is it sometimes hard to believe that Christ will return a second time?

4. In light of your answers to questions 1 and 2, why do you find hope in Christ's second coming?

PARENT PAGE

- Distribute page to parents.

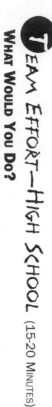

TEAM EFFORT—JUNIOR HIGH/MIDDLE SCHOOL (15-20 Minutes)

ABIDING IN CHRIST

- Give each student a copy of "Abiding in Christ" on page 195 and a pen or pencil, or display a copy using an overhead projector.
- Complete the following activity with the whole group.

To prepare for the second coming of Christ, we are called to abide in Him. Let's take a look at one of the greatest teachings from the ministry of Jesus.

The Vine and the Branches

Read John 15:1-11.

Who: In this teaching who is the

vine—

branches—

gardener (vinedresser)—

What: What is the main concept Jesus is trying to teach us in this section?

Why: Why do you think Jesus brought up the consequences of not bearing fruit (see v. 2)?

How: How do we abide in Christ?

How does this passage apply to my life?

How does this passage apply to the second coming of Christ?

TEAM EFFORT—HIGH SCHOOL (15-20 Minutes)

WHAT WOULD YOU DO?

- Give each student a copy of "What Would You Do?" on page 197 and a pen or pencil.
- Ask students to complete the activity by themselves then spend a few minutes sharing their responses.

Imagine you have just received a special spiritual tip from heaven—Christ will return in 50 years. What would you do?

In five years. What would you do?

In one month. What would you do?

In 24 hours. What would you do?

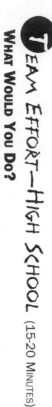

IN THE WORD (25-30 Minutes)

THE SECOND COMING OF CHRIST

- Divide students into groups of three or four.
- Give each student a copy of "The Second Coming of Christ" on pages 199-205 and a pen or pencil, or display a copy using an overhead projector.
- Have the whole group complete Part 1 of the Bible study.
- Have students complete Part II individually and prayerfully.

I. **The Teaching**

Read Matthew 24:1-3. In light of the strong words of Jesus (see vv. 1,2), what is the significance of the disciples' question in verse 3?

Throughout history people have set dates for Christ's return and have been mistaken. What events might deceive the disciples into thinking the end is at hand (see vv. 4-8)?

Before the end comes, what dangers will believers face, and how are we to handle them (see vv. 9-14)?

What can you learn about the "Great Tribulation" from Matthew 24:15-22?

How will we be able to distinguish the false Christ from the true Christ (see vv. 23-31)?

Read Matthew 24:32-51. The time of Christ's coming is discussed in verses 32-41. What can be known about the timing?

What can't be known?

How do the parables of the thief, and the wise and wicked servants (see vv. 42-51) emphasize the importance of living in the light of Christ's return?

II. **The Second Coming and You**

This important teaching of Jesus helps us look at His second coming in the light of three key words: preparedness, watchfulness and faithfulness. You may not be able to figure out all you would like to know about Christ's second coming, but these are definitely action steps you can take to get ready for His return.

A. **Preparedness.**

In light of Matthew 24:36 what can you know about the second coming of Christ?

How does this verse motivate you to prepare for the second coming of Christ?

In the following passages are six ways to prepare for the second coming of Christ. Have people in your group read each section of Scripture and then share how you can prepare for His return.

Proverbs 3:5,6

Isaiah 40:29-31

Micah 6:8

Matthew 16:24

Luke 10:27

Romans 12:1,2

Fold

TEAM EFFORT

ABIDING IN CHRIST

To prepare for the second coming of Christ we are called to abide in Him. Let's take a look at one of the greatest teachings from the ministry of Jesus.

The Vine and the Branches

Read John 15:1-11.

Who: In this teaching who is the

vine—

branches—

gardener (vinedresser)—

What: What is the main concept Jesus is trying to teach us in this section?

Why: Why do you think Jesus brought up the consequences of not bearing fruit (see v. 2)?

How: How do we abide in Christ?

How does this passage apply to my life?

How does this passage apply to the second coming of Christ?

 **TEAM EFFORT**

WHAT WOULD YOU DO?

Imagine you have just received a special spiritual tip from heaven—Christ will return in 50 years. What would you do?

....

....

....

In five years. What would you do?

....

....

....

In one month. What would you do?

....

....

....

In 24 hours. What would you do?

....

....

....

IN THE WORD

THE SECOND COMING OF CHRIST

I. The Teaching

"Jesus left the temple and was walking away when his disciples came up to him to call his attention to its buildings. 'Do you see all these things?' he asked. 'I tell you the truth, not one stone here will be left on another; every one will be thrown down.'

"As Jesus was sitting on the Mount of Olives, the disciples came to him privately. 'Tell us,' they said, 'when will this happen, and what will be the sign of your coming and of the end of the age?'

"Jesus answered: 'Watch out that no one deceives you. For many will come in my name, claiming, "I am the Christ," and will deceive many. You will hear of wars and rumors of wars, but see to it that you are not alarmed. Such things must happen, but the end is still to come. Nation will rise against nation, and kingdom against kingdom. There will be famines and earthquakes in various places. All these are the beginning of birth pains.

"'Then you will be handed over to be persecuted and put to death, and you will be hated by all nations because of me. At that time many will turn away from the faith and will betray and hate each other, and many false prophets will appear and deceive many people. Because of the increase of wickedness, the love of most will grow cold, but he who stands firm to the end will be saved. And this gospel of the kingdom will be preached in the whole world as a testimony to all nations, and then the end will come.

"'So when you see standing in the holy place "the abomination that causes desolation," spoken of through the prophet Daniel—let the reader understand—then let those who are in Judea flee to the mountains. Let no one on the roof of his house go down to take anything out of the house. Let no one in the field go back to get his cloak. How dreadful it will be in those days for pregnant women and nursing mothers! Pray that your flight will not take place in winter or on the Sabbath. For then there will be great distress, unequaled from the beginning of the world until now—and never to be equaled again. If those days had not been cut short, no one would survive, but for the sake of the elect those days will be shortened. At that time if anyone says to you, "Look, here is the Christ!" or "There he is!" do not believe it. For false Christs and false prophets will appear and perform great signs and miracles to deceive even the elect—if that were possible. See, I have told you ahead of time.

"'So if anyone tells you, "There he is, out in the desert," do not go out; or "Here he is, in the inner rooms," do not believe it. For as lightning that comes from the east and is visible even in the west, so will be the coming of the Son of Man. Wherever there is a carcass, there the vultures will gather.

"'Immediately after the distress of those days, "the sun will be darkened, and the moon will not give its light; the stars will fall from the sky, and the heavenly bodies will be shaken."

"'At that time the sign of the Son of Man will appear in the sky, and all the nations of the earth will mourn. They will see the Son of Man coming on the clouds of the sky, with

IN THE WORD

power and great glory. And he will send his angels with a loud trumpet call, and they will gather his elect from the four winds, from one end of the heavens to the other'" (Matthew 24:1-31).

This great passage of Scripture focuses on the teachings of Jesus concerning the destruction of Jerusalem and His second coming. The true issue of Christ's return is not the "hows" or "whens" that fascinate Christians. Rather we must learn to live in the present in the light of the future events.

Read Matthew 24:1-3. In light of the strong words of Jesus (see vv. 1,2), what is the significance of the disciples' question in verse 3?

....

....

Throughout history people have set dates for Christ's return and have been mistaken. What events might deceive the disciples into thinking the end is at hand (see vv.4-8)?

....

....

Before the end comes, what dangers will believers face, and how are we to handle them (see vv. 9-14)?

....

What can you learn about the "Great Tribulation" from Matthew 24:15-22?

....

How will we be able to distinguish the false Christ from the true Christ (see vv. 23-31)?

....

Read Matthew 24:32-51. The time of Christ's coming is discussed in verses 32-41. What can be known about the timing?

....

What can't be known?

....

How do the parables of the thief, and the wise and wicked servants (see vv. 42-51) emphasize the importance of living in the light of Christ's return?

....

....

IN THE WORD

II.   The Second Coming and You

This important teaching of Jesus helps us look at His second coming in the light of three key words: preparedness, watchfulness and faithfulness. You may not be able to figure out all you would like to know about Christ's second coming, but these are definitely action steps you can take to get ready for His return.

A. Preparedness.

In light of Matthew 24:36, what can you know about the second coming of Christ?

....

How does this verse motivate you to prepare for the second coming of Christ?

....

In the following passages are six ways to prepare for the second coming of Christ. Have people in your group read each section of Scripture and then share how you can prepare for His return.

Proverbs 3:5,6

Isaiah 40:29-31

Micah 6:8

Matthew 16:24

Luke 10:27

Romans 12:1,2

B. Watchfulness.

"To live without watchfulness invites disaster. A thief does not send a letter saying when he is going to burgle a house; his principal weapon in his nefarious undertakings is surprise; therefore a householder who has valuables in his house must maintain a constant guard. But to get this picture right, we must remember that the watchdog of the Christian for the coming of Christ is not that of terror-stricken fear and shivering apprehension: it is the watching of eager expectation for the coming of glory and joy."[2]

What does it mean in practical terms to have an attitude of watchfulness?

....

Read 1 Thessalonians 5:1-11. How will the Lord come (see v. 7)?

....

List the suggestions found in verses 4-11 that will help you prepare for the coming of the Lord.

....

Which of the listed suggestions do you need to work on the most? Circle your answer. What specifically will you do to work on this area of your Christian life?

....

....

N THE WORD

C. Faithfulness.

Faithfulness is one of the key ingredients in living a consistent Christian life. The Scripture tells us that the rewards of faithfulness are great. What is the reward for the faithful servant in the parable found in Matthew 24:45-51? What is the reward for the unfaithful servant?

....

On the scale below, place a mark indicating your general level of faithfulness to God.

Faithfulness

1	2	3	4	5	6	7	8	9	10
Never faithful		Seldom faithful		Sometimes faithful		Usually faithful			Always faithful

So What?

What will you do to improve your level of faithfulness?

....

....

1. Some of the questions in this section are taken from an excellent workbook by Stephen and Jacalyn Eyre, *Matthew: Being Discipled by Jesus*, (Downers Grove, Ill.: InterVarsity Press, 1987), pp. 65-66. Used by permission.

2. William Barclay, *The Gospel of Matthew, Vol. II, The Daily Study Bible Series* (Philadelphia, Penn.: Westminster Press, 1975), p. 317. Used by permission.

THINGS TO THINK ABOUT

1. Do you think our world is getting better or worse with each generation? Why?

....

2. What are your greatest fears about the future?

....

3. Why is it sometimes hard to believe that Christ will return a second time?

....

4. In light of your answers to questions 1 and 2, why do you find hope in Christ's second coming?

....

....

PARENT PAGE

FAITHFULNESS

One of our responses to prepare for the second coming of Christ must be remaining faithful to Him. Here's an inspiring story about faithfulness.

One of the bleakest chapters in Northern Ireland's prison history took place from roughly 1979 to 1981, when terrorist inmates of Belfast's Maze Prison embarked upon a series of prison strikes to frustrate the British government and gain world publicity for their cause.

Prisoners on one such strike, "the dirty protest," refused to wash, refused to wear clothing, refused to leave their cells. Covered only by a blanket with a ragged hole cut out for the head, they sat on the concrete floor. They smeared their excrement on the walls and rinsed their hands with their urine. Their hair and beards grew long and knotted, streaked with filth.

Though the prisoners grew accustomed to the incredible stench, officers often vomited and fainted. Visitors were nonexistent.

That is, except for Gladys Blackburne.

On Christmas Eve, 1980, Gladys Blackburne was having tea in her small Belfast flat. A retired schoolteacher in her mid-sixties, Miss Blackburne was an inch shy of five feet. With gently curled gray hair, pearls, and sensible shoes, she had a determined way about her.

Miss Blackburne had long taken Northern Ireland's civil unrest personally, asking God to show her what she could do to honor Him in a land where 'the name of Jesus was being dragged in the gutter.' And she had been doing what she believed God had required of her: to be the best citizen she could in her small, troubled nation, and to show the love of Christ to those in need.

Session 11 "The Holy Spirit"
Date...

PARENT PAGE

But Gladys Blackburne was not a person to take God's direction lightly. As she put on her coat and gloves, she prayed for the grace to handle what she would find at the Maze.

She hitched a ride to the prison and cleared the laborious security checks. Before she got to the dirty protesters, however, a Christian prison officer took her aside. "There's a lad in a different wing who's asking a lot of questions about Christianity," he said. "Why don't you visit him first?"

Thus it was that Gladys Blackburne spent her Christmas Eve, as she would the next several years, in the Maze Prison among the inmates. And thus it was that she met Chips, a young inmate who had studied terrorism, Marxism, fascism and atheism, finding no answers. Gladys Blackburne, sitting there on a prison chair, her feet barely touching the floor, told Chips about Jesus Christ—born nearly 2,000 years earlier to heal the hearts of those who were broken. And later that Christmas Eve, while Gladys Blackburne went on to sit with the dirty protesters and lead them in Christmas carols, Chips committed his life to Jesus Christ.[1]

What made Miss Blackburne such a faithful person?

....

....

....

What can we do as a family to remain faithfully prepared for the return of Jesus Christ?

....

....

....

Note:

1. Chuck Colson, "Jubilee," *A Newsletter of Prison Fellowship*, (December 1987): 7.

Session 12 "The Second Coming"

Date......................................

Add a New Member to Your Youth Staff.

Jim Burns is president of the National Institute of Youth Ministry.

Meet Jim Burns. He won't play guitar and he doesn't do windows, but he will take care of your programming needs. That's because his new curriculum, **YouthBuilders Group Bible Studies** is a comprehensive program designed to take your group through their high school years. (If you have junior high kids in your group, **YouthBuilders** works for them too.)

For less than $6 a month you'll get Jim Burns's special recipe of high-involvement, discussion-oriented, Bible-centered studies. It's the next generation of Bible curriculum for youth—and with Jim on your staff, you'll be free to spend more time one-on-one with the kids in your group.

Here are some of YouthBuilders' hottest features:

- Reproducible pages—one book fits your whole group
- Wide appeal—big groups, small groups—even adjusts to fit jr. high/high school groups
- Hits home—special section to involve parents with every session of the study
- Interactive Bible discovery—geared to help young people find answers themselves
- Cheat sheets—a Bible *Tuck-In*™ with all the session information on a single page
- Flexible format—perfect for Sunday mornings, midweek youth meetings, or camps and retreats
- Three studies in one—each study has three, four-session modules examining critical life choices.

The Word on Sex, Drugs & Rock 'N' Roll
Gives youth a biblical framework for making good choices in life. ISBN 08307.16424

The Word on Prayer and the Devotional Life
Help high school youth get closer to God by getting a grip on prayer. ISBN 08307.16432

The Word on the Basics of Christianity
Here are the foundational truths of Christianity, presented in an active format. ISBN 08307.16440

The Word on Being a Leader, Serving Others & Sharing Your Faith
Students can serve God and each other by taking an active role in leadership. ISBN 08307.16459

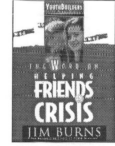

The Word on Helping Friends in Crisis
Young people can discover what God's Word says about crisis issues and how to help others. ISBN 08307.16467

A Push-Button Course for Junior High.

 r. High Builders are all-in-one programs that help kids put their faith in action. Each book in the series includes 13 Bible studies, dozens of games and activities as well as clip art to illustrate your handouts—all you have to do is warm up the copier!

Jr. High Builders titles include:
- Christian Basics (ISBN 08307.16963)
- Christian Relationships (ISBN 08307.17013)
- Symbols of Christ (ISBN 08307.17021)
- Power of God (ISBN 08307.17048)
- Faith in Action (ISBN 08307.17056)
- Peace, Love and Truth (ISBN 08307.17064)
- Lifestyles of the Not-so-Famous from the Bible (ISBN 08307.17099)

These are only a few of the YouthBuilders and Jr. High Builders studies available. For a complete list, contact your Gospel Light supplier.

Gospel Light

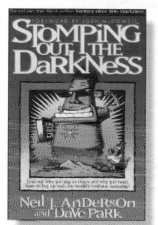

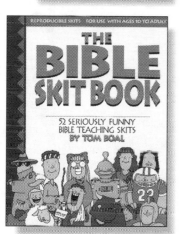

What in the world is *NIYM*?

A.) The Neurotically Inclined Yo-Yo Masters

B.) The Neatest Incidental Yearbook Mystery

C.) The Natural Ignition Yields of Marshmallows

D.) The National Institute of Youth Ministry

If you deliberately picked *A, B,* or *C* you're the reason Jim Burns started NIYM! If you picked *D,* you can go to the next page. In any case, you could learn more about NIYM. Here are some IQ score-raisers:

Jim Burns started NIYM to:
• Meet the growing needs of training and equipping youth workers and parents
• Develop excellent resources and events for young people—in the U.S. and internationally
• Empower young people and their families to make wise decisions and experience a vital Christian lifestyle.

NIYM can make a difference in your life and enhance your youth work skills through these special events:

Institutes—These consist of week-long, in-depth small-group training sessions for youth workers.

Trainer of Trainees—NIYM will train you to train others. You can use this training with your volunteers, parents and denominational events. You can go through the certification process and become an official NIYM associate. (No, you don't get a badge or decoder ring).

International Training—Join NIYM associates to bring youth ministry to kids and adults around the world. (You'll learn meanings to universal words like "yo!" and "hey!")

Custom Training—These are special training events for denominational groups, churches, networks, colleges and seminaries.

Parent Forums—We'll come to your church or community with two incredible hours of learning, interaction and fellowship. It'll be fun finding out who makes your kids tick!

Youth Events—Dynamic speakers, interaction and drama bring a powerful message to kids through a fun and fast-paced day. Our youth events include: This Side Up, Radical Respect, Surviving Adolescence and Peer Leadership.

For brain food or a free information packet about the National Institute of Youth Ministry, write to:

NIYM

P.O. Box 4374 • San Clemente, CA 92674

Tel: (714) 498-4418 • Fax: (714) 498-0037 • NIYMin@aol.com